D0044916

Erma Bombeck's books have established her as one of America's bestselling, best-loved humorists. It is well known that Mrs. Bombeck is dynamic, attractive, and into asparagus. A noted think-thin activist, she was once arrested for throwing a butterscotch sundae off a cliff without remorse. "A doozy, written in impeccable Bombeck style ... While we are Saran–ing and sweating and TM–ing our way toward ourselves, Erma is watching. What she sees is hilarious."
                    —*DES MOINES REGISTER*

"Reading this book is like eating popcorn —you can't stop—and you don't really want to."
                    —*Associated Press*

Aunt Erma's Cope Book

HOW TO GET FROM MONDAY TO FRIDAY ... IN 12 DAYS

by Erma Bombeck

FAWCETT CREST • NEW YORK

A Fawcett Crest Book
Published by Ballantine Books

Copyright © 1979 by Erma Bombeck

All rights reserved under International and Pan-American
Copyright Conventions. Published in the United States by
Ballantine Books, a division of Random House, Inc., New
York, and simultaneously in Canada by Random House of
Canada Limited, Toronto.

ISBN 0-449-20937-7

This edition published by arrangement with
McGraw Hill Book Company

Featured alternate selection of the Book-of-the-Month Club
Dual selection of the Cooking and Crafts Book Club

Manufactured in the United States of America

First Fawcett Crest Edition: October 1980
First Ballantine Books Edition: August 1983
Fourth Printing: May 1985

Contents

For Betsy Bombeck, Andy Bombeck, and
  Matt Bombeck

If I blow it raising them . . .
nothing else I do will matter very much.

Aunt Erma's Cope Book

1

How Do I Like Me So Far?

All the way to Jill's cocktail party, I had that feeling of exhilaration . . . like when your gelatin mold comes out in one piece or you grab the door of a pay booth in the rest room just before it slams shut.

For the first time in a long time, my life was coming together. And it felt good. I no longer anguished over what I looked like. I could pass a mirror without looking at my neck and being reminded I hadn't made homemade chicken soup in a while. I had come to grips with domesticity and no longer believed that unmade beds caused shortness of breath.

My husband's infatuation with Angie Dickinson had wound down and I noted the same ecstasy he used to reserve for her pictures now appeared in his face whenever his soup was hot.

All three kids were not only speaking to us, but our twenty-four-year-old daughter openly displayed a curiosity as to how to turn on the stove.

I was becoming more assertive, refusing to "honk when I loved Jesus." I no longer inhaled around my smoker friends.

The pressures of child raising were easing off. I stopped feeling guilty for my children's colds, their overbites, or for that matter allowing our daughter to be born without pompon hands.

I stopped eating chocolates in the closet, dedicating my life to putting toilet seats down, or pretending to feel sorry for women wearing industrial-strength bras.

In my awkward way, I was reentering

the human race after twenty years of Edith Bunkering it.

My husband disliked parties. He called them the Varicose Olympics where people stood around all night talking about their dog's hysterectomies and eating bait off of little round crackers. If our social life were left up to him, the high spot of my week would have been watching the hot wax drip down on our car at the Car Wash.

My eyes fairly danced as we entered the room and I spotted my old friend Phyllis. I hadn't seen her in ages.

"Phyllis!" I shouted. "How long has it been? Do you still bowl with the League on Tuesdays?"

Phyllis set down her glass without smiling. "Bowl? That was only a transference of aggression to keep me from dealing with my realities head-on."

"C'mon," I laughed, "eighty-six wasn't *that* bad a score."

"You remember how I used to have anxiety attacks when I emptied the sweeper bag? Well, the bottom line was I was in a crisis situation I couldn't handle . . . which is what you'd expect from a Gemini, right? So, I began to read self-help books to raise my consciousness level. Right now I'm reading *Sensual Needlepoint* by Candy Summers. She also wrote *Erotic Leftovers* and *Kinky Lint*."

"*Sensual Needlepoint?*" I said, gulping my drink.

"Believe me," she whispered. "You will never make another French knot for as long as you live. By the way, you belong to the Cope-of-the-Month-Club Guild, don't you?" I shook my head. "Every month you get a self-help book on how to improve yourself. Of course you've read *Fear of Landing* by Erika Wrong and Dr. Dryer's new book, *I Hope the Sexual Revolution Doesn't End Before I'm Drafted?*"

"Phyllis," I said, "what's happened to you? You used to be so shallow!"

She ignored my comment. "Incidentally, why are you paranoid about kissing people hello?"

"I am not paranoid."

"Yes, you are. When you approached me just now, you extended your hand. You really are inhibited."

"I'm not inhibited. I didn't kiss you because I've been eating Roquefort."

"When was the last time you told Erma how you felt about her?"

I looked over the crowd. "Erma who?"

"Erma YOU, that's who."

"You know I don't like to talk about me in front of myself. It's embarrassing."

"I knew you'd masquerade your true feelings behind cheap jokes. It's just like you to make light of something serious. But frankly, I don't know how much longer you can sit by and watch the rest of the world probe into their inner minds and understand the heights of man's nobility and the depths of his depravity."

"That's beautiful. Where did you read that?"

"In the *National Enquirer* in the express lane at the supermarket. Do you know what's wrong with you?" she asked, leaning closer. "Sex! It should be apparent

15

to you that it's time you got in touch with your feelings. Get to know yourself. We're moving into the 1980s, sweetie, where sex dominates everything we do. You and your husband are probably just plain bored with one another. It happens in a lot of marriages. You just take one another for granted after a while."

"Phyllis, I do not believe we are having this conversation. You're the one who was too shy to tell anyone you were pregnant. You told everyone you had 'something in the oven.' You raised children who thought it took nine months to bake a pie!"

"Well, things are different now," said Phyllis. "I know that sex is something you have to work on in a marriage. You need Clarabelle Sweet."

"You mean the author of *The Sub-Total Woman?* I think I've heard of her."

"HEARD OF HER!" shouted Phyllis shrilly. "Are you serious? Women haven't been so excited about a book since *Sex Causes Fatness* came out. You know the one where the author said that making love burns up fewer calories than throwing a Frisbee? I tell you what. I'll loan you my copy if you promise to return it."

"I do not need help from *The Sub-Total Woman*."

"When was the last time you bathed with your husband?"

"When we washed the dog."

"Do you share your husband's interest in sports? Do you create a mood for romance? Have you ever made sheets out of Astroturf?"

Phyllis was whacko. No doubt about it. I eased away and observed my husband across the room. For a man going through his metallic age (silver hair, gold teeth, and lead bottom) he did cut quite a figure. I watched him as he was joined by a girl with solar hair who was so animated I thought her face would break. As I turned, I caught Phyllis looking at me. She smiled and yelled, "Trust me! *The Sub-Total Woman* will change your life!"

2

The Sub-Total Woman

Clarabelle Sweet had been on all the talk shows touting her book, *The Sub-Total Woman.*

Clarabelle had long black hair and said things like "When a man's got cream in the refrigerator at home, he won't go out looking for two-percent butterfat."

She appeared on a sex-theme show with Merv Griffin, explained how 350 boxes of gelatin could change your life on Donahue, and made a three-bean salad on Dinah! (The garbanzo beans spelled out L–O–V–E.)

There was no doubt in my mind she had

a Spanish doll nestled among the satin pillows on her bed. I figured that out after reading the Compatible Quiz.

At the beginning, it bothered me to know, without taking it, that I'd flunk. And somehow, after thirty years of marriage and three children, I didn't want to know that my husband and I had been incompatible.

But I couldn't resist it.

"Post Scripts to 'I DO' "
(Score yourself ten points for each correct answer)

• You and your husband are alone in a cabin for the first time since your marriage. He is nibbling on your ear. Do you (a) nibble back or (b) tell him the toilet is running?

• Your husband comes home unexpectedly in the middle of the afternoon. Do you (a) slip into something suggestive and make him an offer he can't refuse or (b) leave him there while you take the car and go to a food-processor demonstration?

• Your husband invites you to go to a convention where you will share only your evenings together. Do you (a) get a babysitter and go or (b) regard it as a great time to stay at home and paint the bedroom?

• Check your husband's driver's license. Under SEX does he list (a) male or (b) only during a full moon?

• After a long, hard day your husband drags in feeling tired and listless. Do you (a) massage his feet with witch hazel or (b) tell him all he needs is a good laxative?

• When you've had a bad day and need tenderness and understanding does your husband (a) wrap you in his arms and tell you he adores you or (b) read the paper and absentmindedly scratch you behind your ear and call you the dog's name?

I didn't have to score myself. The results were rather obvious. I had become a woman who said "I do" but didn't from the day she got her first set of car keys.

I didn't pamper my husband and I didn't serve his needs. Maybe Phyllis was right. Maybe we had fallen into a rut at a time when we needed it most.

When I thought about it, the last time he put his arms around me in a movie, I had a miniature bus caught in my throat from a Cracker-Jack box.

I'd feel like a fool padding around after him. We weren't demonstrative people. Never had been. On the other hand, what if someday he developed a craving for 2-percent butterfat? If Clarabelle Sweet's husband called her from the office every day just to pant into the phone for a minute and a half maybe it was worth it.

The next morning my husband called from the bathroom, "What's this?"

On the mirror in lipstick, I had written "65 MILLION WOMEN WANT MY HUSBAND."

"It's just a reminder, dear, how lucky I am to have you."

He studied the mirror carefully and said, "Name names."

"Don't get testy. Clarabelle Sweet says if women treated their husbands better they wouldn't wander."

"Who is Clarabelle Sweet and where am I going?"

"She's going to save our marriage. Here is your shaver, your bath towel, your soap, and your shampoo."

"Where's my rubber duck?" he asked irritably.

"And your comb, your deodorant, your clean shirt, and your trousers. Here, let me put that lid down for you."

"GET OUT OF THE BATHROOM," he yelled through clenched teeth.

Looking back on it, I never knew how being subservient could be so unappreciated. When I tried to spoonfeed him his cereal, he stopped eating. When I measured out his dental floss, he left the bathroom. When I lit a match under his chin, he blew it out and snarled "I don't smoke, remember?"

As I was standing in the driveway holding his attaché case, he said "And lay off the vanilla."

"I'll call you at work," I said huskily. "Try to come home early."

When he was gone, I went back to *The Sub-Total Woman* for assurance. It appeared on page 110. "In a survey of 10,000 males," it read, "almost half of them said they cheated on their wives and most said they wanted or needed some physical display of affection.

"Given a list of qualities for a partner, they arranged them in the following order:

1. A woman with concern for my needs
2. Sincerity
3. Affection
4. Intelligence
5. Self-confidence
6. Sexuality
7. Sense of humor."

It read more like a Boy Scout handbook.

Just after lunch, I went to the phone

and dialed my husband's office. The wait seemed interminable. Finally, his secretary answered and said she would put me through.

"Hello," I said, trying to make my voice sound throaty. "Could you come home early?"

"Whatsa matter?" he asked. "Do you have a dental appointment?"

"Come home early and you can have your way with me."

"Hang on a second. Another call is coming through," he said, and PUT ME ON HOLD!

I hung up the phone and went back to Clarabelle's book. "Jar your husband out of his lethargy by meeting him at the door dressed in something outrageous like a cheerleader . . . a bunny . . . or a slave girl."

A costume. Was she serious? Even at Halloween I just put brown grocery bags over the kids' heads, cut two eyes in them, and told them to tell everyone their mother was having surgery. I wasn't good at costumes.

I went through all the closets and the only thing I could come up with was a pair of the boys' football pants, jersey, and helmet. I felt about as sensuous as a bride with a lip full of Novocain, but when you're trying to save a marriage you have to go for it.

When I heard the car in the driveway, I flung open the front door and yelled, "It's a scoreless game so far."

The washer repairman didn't say anything for a couple of minutes. His eyes never met mine. He just stared at the floor and mumbled, "It says here on the work sheet that your dryer won't heat up."

I cleared my throat. "Right, come in. The dryer is next to the washer behind the louvered doors." Neither of us spoke. The only sound was of my cleats clicking on the terrazzo tile. He worked in silence and I disappeared in the other end of the house.

As I wrote him a check, he took it, shook his head, and said, "I hope your team wins, lady."

I got out of the football uniform and into a dress. Who was I kidding? I wasn't ready for the Sub-Total Super Bowl and I knew it.

I couldn't even create the atmosphere for it. We ate dinner between *Family Feud* and *Name That Tune*. The kids fanned in and out like a revolving door. The only way you could get them to turn their stereos down was to tell them you could hear the words. There were clothes to fold, purchases to discuss, decisions to be made and, of course, the electronic sleeping pill—the parade of sports.

I never realized what a holding pattern we were in until I tried to massage my husband's neck and he said, "I'll save you time. My billfold's on the dresser."

I returned to folding clothes when about eleven or so we both heard the smoke alarm go off in our bedroom.

We rushed back to see my sheer red nightgown smoking from the heat of the lightbulb on the lamp.

"Why is your nightgown draped over the lamp?" asked my husband evenly.

"I am creating a mood."

"For a disaster movie?"

"It was supposed to give the room a sexy, sensuous feeling."

"Open the window. If it gets any sexier in here, I'm going to pass out."

It was an hour or so before the smoke cleared and we could go to bed.

"Did you call me today or did I imagine it?" he asked.

"I called."

"What did you want?"

"I wanted to tell you to come home early and you could have your way with me."

"You should have left a message." He yawned and crawled into bed.

I turned on the bathroom light. The mirror still reflected "65 MILLION WOMEN WANT MY HUSBAND." I took out a deodorant stick and wrote under it WHY?

The simple fact was we couldn't be something we had never been. We were too old to change.

Besides, according to experts we were going through the best phase of our lives.

The children were grown and I didn't have to cope with rainbows over the crib and knotted shoestrings. The house carried a preinflation 9-percent mortgage. And I had Mayva. Mayva was my best friend, who never went on a diet when I was fat, never told me the truth when I begged for it, and when my husband bought me a vegetable slicer for my birthday never said something stupid like "At least he doesn't drink or play around like a lot of husbands."

When Mayva saw Clarabelle Sweet's book on the hall table she nearly flipped. "You're reading *The Sub-Total Woman*? You can't be serious. Don't you know that converting your Donny Osmond night light into a strobe isn't going to turn your life around? I know what's wrong with you. You're like a lot of married couples who are floundering around in a traditional marriage that doesn't exist any more. No one paddles around waiting on one another these days. Things should be equal between you. Each of you should have a sense of self. Do you know what I'm saying?"

"No more books, Mayva."

"Listen, Pam McMeal and Richard McMeal's book *Is There a Draft in Your Open Marriage?* really spells it out. Answer me this. When was the last time you and Bill took separate vacations?"

"When we left the kids with Mother."

"You should be at a time of your life when you have an open and an honest relationship. No one dominates and no one is submissive any more. You share. You grow. You leave behind the years of sitting under your children and develop an awareness of what is going on in the world. And heaven help you if you awake one morning to discover your husband has outgrown you."

I didn't say anything for a minute, then asked, "What made you say that, Mayva?"

"It's not important," she said.

"It is! You know something you're not telling me. What is it?"

"It's just that the other night when all of us were talking and Bill mentioned the Gross National Product you said, 'Nothing is more gross than commercials for feminine hygiene products.'"

I stiffened. "I suppose you know of a more gross commercial product?"

"Read the McMeals' book," she said. "I'll drop it off tomorrow. Believe me, it'll change your life."

A woman with twenty-six boxes of lime gelatin couldn't afford to close her mind to suggestions.

3

Is There a Draft in Your Open Marriage?

My Son, Jaws II, had a habit that drove me crazy. He'd walk to the refrigerator-freezer and fling both doors open and stand there until the hairs in his nose iced up. After surveying two hundred dollars' worth of food in varying shapes and forms he would declare loudly "There's nothing to eat."

I used to react to that remark like a gauntlet thrown down or an attack on my honor. The remark no longer held a challenge for me. I sat at the table and continued to read my book.

"Are you reading another book on marriage?" he asked.

"What's the matter with that?"

"Nothing," he said, then added, "There's something I always wondered. How come you and Dad never lived together before tying the knot?"

I said, "Are you crazy? We got married because we didn't know one another well enough to live together."

The remark was ludicrous and we both knew it. The truth is, in a world of "limited arrangements," "meaningful relationships," and "marital concepts" his father and I were dinosaurs.

We had never negotiated the old contract, never dropped an option on one another, never comparison-shopped. We not only hadn't a clue as to where one another was coming from . . . we didn't know where we were going until one of the kids brought home the car.

We must have seemed weird in a world where young people met in a line to see *Superman,* made a commitment to one another by the intermission, and dissolved the relationship between ordering a pizza and picking it up.

I closed the McMeals' book. It was more frightening than *Future Shock*. They wrote that one out of every three marriages ended in divorce and that 75 percent of all the existing ones were in big trouble. The rest of it made marriage sound as exciting as a yogurt orgy.

After thirty years of marriage, I felt like a truss in a drugstore window—dependable, serviceable, and down-right orthopedic.

Were married people an endangered species? In time would they talk of the days when men and women roamed the earth in wedlock as matched sets? Was it possible that some day cohabital living would be the sanctified relationship and marriage would be frowned on by society?

I could just see my son coming home from school one day . . . his shirt torn, blood around his mouth, sneaking to his room to avoid a confrontation.

When cornered, he'd finally admit he had a fight on the playground.

"But why?" I'd ask.

"Because Rich said . . . he accused you and Dad . . . he said you and Dad were MARRIED!"

"And what did you say?"

"I told him he was a creep. Then he said everyone in school knew it and if you weren't, then how come my last name is the same as yours? Is it true?"

When I finally nodded my head, I could see him shouting angrily, "Why can't you and Dad live together like everyone else's parents?"

I'd explain: "I'm sorry. Your father and I never wanted to embarrass you. Do you think we liked sneaking around checking into hotels *with* luggage? Wearing my wedding ring on a chain around my neck? Pinching one another in front of your friends to make them think we were not married? I'm glad the charade is over. I'm sick of going to Marriage Encounter meetings in separate cars."

When pressed as to why we did it, I'd explain we wanted to try marriage to see if it got on our nerves and if it didn't work out, we'd just quietly get a divorce and no one would get hurt that way.

I felt a chill. He was standing in front of the double doors to the refrigerator-freezer again. "What's in this yellow box?" he asked, ripping the top off with his teeth.

It was too late. The film was in his mouth.

When I thought about it, our marriage wasn't exactly made in heaven by a long shot. We had our disagreements. A little ventilation couldn't hurt. The McMeals advised couples to give one another room in their marriage to breathe and to develop as persons. They said couples should try to be more independent of one another.

As a woman who was up to her Astro-turf in football, I'd buy that. How many years had I put in trudging out to the stadium every week to endure a two-and-one-half-hour sleeping pill?

Sure, men are supposed to get an emotional high out of football. But did anyone care that I've gotten bigger emotional highs out of getting a piece of dental floss caught in my teeth?

I got so bored I used to play games with myself.

I played the Fashion Alphabet with Peggy Ronstadt for a whole season. We used to alternate naming a style worn by other women in the stands from Accordion pleats and Blouses to Yokes and Zippers. The first one who couldn't come up with a style for a letter was penalized by watching the game until a first down was made.

The Hot-Dog-Cola Caper was always good for an hour or so. Disguising my voice, I'd yell down and order a hot dog and a cola from the vendor at the end of the row. Without an eye leaving the game, people passed it down an entire row of 138 people. When it got to the end they'd pass it back to the next row. I'd watch to see how many rows the hot dog and cola covered before someone finally ate it.

Another one Peggy and I always played was Stump the Fans. We'd establish a pool of a couple of bucks and the first one to figure out what the band was trying to spell out on the playing field won. (I once won eight dollars when I correctly identified a tuba player as an anchovy on a field of pizza.)

I wondered what my husband would say if I announced next Saturday afternoon that I wasn't going to the football game with him. I might just find out how secure our marriage really is.

When I talked with my neighbor Lynda, she looked shocked. "You can't be serious. You have a chance to go to a football game with your husband and you're trying to get out of it."

"What's wrong with that?"

"I'd give anything if my Jim watched football. Why, there's no healthier sport for a man in this world than a football game. Sitting out there in the bleachers with a thermos of hot coffee and a blanket over your knees, sharing . . ."

"What's the matter with you?" I asked. "You're the one who really got ticked off when you had to hire a Goodyear blimp to tell Jim you delivered him a son."

"I know. Those were the good old days. Now, every Saturday he gets up, fills his thermos, and races toward the stadium. All he talks about are the tight ends, the line and the backfield in motion. And the kickers. He raves about the kickers."

"I thought you said he didn't like football."

"He doesn't. All he watches are the pompon girls. Fifty of them with spaghetti legs, concave stomachs, and their inflatable made-in-Japan chests. Last Saturday when the team came on the field he said, 'Let's get something to drink while the game is being played, so we'll make it back in time for halftime.' I tell you, they're ruining the sport."

"Oh c'mon, Lynda," I said, "no one can stamp out football. It's like head colds and Doris Day . . . it will be with us always, whether we go or not. And don't tell me you wouldn't like to rewrite your marriage contract if you were given a chance."

I wrote down just a few things yesterday that really bug me about our marriage. I'm going to pin it to his pillow. Listen to this.

Takes his leisure suit . . . literally.

Puts toilet paper on the spindle with the paper coming from UNDER the roll just to annoy me.

Lied to me about ultrasuede coming from an endangered species that would ultimately cause an imbalance of nature.

Never shares with me things from the office told to him in confidence that he has sworn never to divulge.

Agrees to shop with me, then leans against the wall like he is awaiting gum surgery.

Said publicly my upper arms looked like cloverleaf rolls.

"Good Lord, that was ten years ago," said Lynda.

"There is no statute of limitations on fat-arms jokes. And in addition to all of that, he puts down my soap operas."

The latter had been a bone of contention for years. And I didn't know why. I only watched one, *The Wild and the Spoiled.*

Of course it was pure fiction. I mean, where else could you see a man who told his wife he loved her . . . with the lights on? But it held my attention.

Soaps had really changed in the years I'd been watching them. They had gone from innocent bits of fluff where the heroine served a lot of coffee and romped through a full-term pregnancy in three weeks, to abortion, alcoholism, incest, cohabital living, drugs, homosexuality, and talking back to mothers.

The heroine of *The Wild and the Spoiled* was named Erogenique. If you couldn't make it in this world with a name like Erogenique you just weren't trying.

It boggled my mind to imagine what Erogenique did on her days off *The Wild and the Spoiled.* I used to fantasize that the two of us were roommates in a New York apartment and were as different as night and day. She would rush in breathless every evening, prattling on about a new conquest who would pick her up within the hour and would I be a love and let him in.

Every time she did this, she lost her newfound desire to me. It was always the same. He would stand in the doorway; struck numb by my wholesomeness. He could have had my roommate (who didn't have a dead spot on her entire body), but he wanted me who was content to sit at home and needlepoint a flag.

When he could stand it no longer, he would reach out to pull me close—at which point I would back off and shout "If you want someone with touch control, get yourself a microwave oven."

I wondered how Erogenique would have handled thirty years with the NFL, then answered my own question.

A couple of weeks after I had decided to open my marriage to drafts, while I was watching *The Wild and the Spoiled* Lynda appeared at the door and said, "I'm dying to ask. What happened when you told your husband you weren't going to go to the football games with him?"

"He said, 'Okay.' "

"That's it?"

"That's it. Shhh, Erogenique is trying to compromise the funeral director at her stepfather's funeral."

Her sister Emma spoke: "You know the trouble with you, Erogenique, is you don't have a good feeling about yourself. You could never have a relationship with anyone because your independence has made you destructive. You don't like anyone else and you don't like yourself because there is nothing to love. You fill me with loathing and disgust!"

"Did you hear that?" I asked. "I think she's got a point. Erogenique doesn't like Erogenique. She doesn't have a good feeling toward herself."

"That's the trouble," yawned Lynda. "Everybody is trying to make you feel good about yourself. You can't be mediocre in this world any more. You have to be perfection itself. Look at that! Even the commercials are pitching it."

We watched in silence as a housewife

called Mildred was being interviewed in the supermarket. The interviewer asked Mildred whether her husband preferred potatoes or stuffing with his chicken.

Mildred, who had given birth to his children, drunk out of the same bathroom glass and caught his colds, said without blinking an eye, "Potatoes. My husband would definitely choose potatoes."

When they interviewed the husband in the next scene he said, "Stuffing. I would definitely choose stuffing."

In the third scene his wife is visibly shaken as she stammers, "I didn't know . . . but from here on in I will definitely serve stuffing."

I turned to Lynda. "Gosh, I don't know," I said, my eyes glistening with excitement. "I think Bill would have chosen stuffing. What about Jim?"

Lynda looked at me tiredly. "Who cares?" she said. "I could serve him Top of the Stove Moose and he would have had it for lunch. If Mildred had any sense, she'd give that dim bulb stuffing all right . . . right up his nose!"

"What are you so upset about?" I asked.

"I'm upset because I'm sick and tired of sitting around being told how to exhaust myself and pop iron tablets. We're all being manipulated, you know. I read all about how traps are laid for consumers in a new book called *Fear of Buying*. Supermarkets are like mazes, children drive you crazy to buy things they see on TV, and advertisers have us believing the only time we experience ecstasy is when we drink coffee, take showers, chew gum, or smell laundry. I've got the book if you'd like to read it."

I shook my head.

"It's a real eye-opener."

Later that day I was emptying the waste basket in the bedroom when I saw my list of complaints for the new open marriage contract. Someone had wrapped gum in it.

Maybe I was being manipulated . . . but it beat being ignored.

4

Fear of Buying

To tell you the truth, I had never thought a lot about what motivated me to buy.

As Bob Newhart once remarked about his friendship with Don Rickles, "Someone has to do it."

I did as I was told. I was fussy about my peanut butter, fought cavities, became depressed over yellow wax buildup, and buried my head in my laundry like I had just witnessed God.

I personally knew women who carried a quart bottle of laxative, three pounds of Mountain-Grown coffee, and a complete line of feminine products in their handbags. I never did that.

But we all believed. We believed if we converted to all the products that marched before our eyes, we could be the best, the sexiest, the freshest, the cleanest, the thinnest, the smartest, and the first in our block to be regular.

Purchasing for the entire family was the most important thing I had to do.

In 1969, a man walked on the moon. Big deal! That same year I found a pair of gym shoes that would make my son jump higher than a basketball hoop.

A birth-control pill was perfected that would make an impact on the population of the entire world. Hosanna! I discovered a little man for my toilet bowl that cleaned as it flushed.

Our government was involved in a cover-up. So what? It was enough for me to know that while I was in bed reading, my oven was cleaning itself.

My children dominated my buying

habits and I knew it. They could sing beer commercials before their eyes could focus.

I remember one day standing in front of a cupboard with eleven boxes of half-eaten cereal ranging from Fortified Blinkies and Captain Sugar to Toasted Wriggles, Heap of Honey, and Cavity Krispies. They didn't snap, crackle, or pop any more. They just lay there on the shelf turning stale year after year.

I told the kids I had had it and there would be no more new cereal brought into the house until we cleaned up what we already had. I even did some fast arithmetic and figured out that a box of Bloated Oats had cost me a total of $116.53. This included repairing my tooth, which I chipped on a nuclear submarine in the bottom of the box, throwing part of the cereal to the birds in the snow, necessitating antibiotics, and the cost of packing, shipping, and crating it through three moves.

Eventually we polished off every box, only to be confronted with the most important decision we had ever made as a family: the selection of a new box of cereal.

I personally favored Bran Brittles because they made you regular and offered an African violet as a premium.

One child wanted Chock Full of Soggies because they turned your teeth purple.

Another wanted Jungle Jollies because they had no nutritional value whatsoever.

We must have spent twenty minutes in the cereal aisle before we decided on Mangled Wheat Bits because "when eaten as an after-school snack, will give you X-Ray vision."

Since the children were grown, we were still under the spell of the hard sell. I had gotten used to buying them Christmas presents that (a) I couldn't spell, (b) had no idea what they were used for, and (c) leaked grease.

Since they were older, their letters at Christmas were a far cry from Christmas past when they wrote "Dear Santa: Please leave me a new doll and a bike."

Mesmerized by some commercial, I

would get a list from them that spelled out their desire right down to the catalogue number.

"An RF–60 FM stereo wireless radio chamber. Ask for Frank; five percent off list price if you pay cash."

Or "273 auto thyristor bounce flash 9–90 with head tilt for the big gift and for the stocking stuffer a couple of rolls of EX 135–30 Ektachrome ASA 64–19."

I didn't think too much about *Fear of Buying* until one night after I had lugged in twelve bags of groceries (while everyone else hid out in the john) and my husband poked through the bags and said, "What are we having for dinner? A pot of mums, a room deodorizer, a bag of charcoal, or an encyclopedia?"

That tore it. I slammed down the bag and said, "Is that the thanks I get for taking care of this family's needs? It's a jungle out there and I go into it every week . . . inexperienced people driving shopping carts, kids throwing things into your basket, coupons to clip, lists to juggle, labels to read, fruits to pinch, toilet paper to squeeze, sales to find—and as for the encyclopedias, YOU try to find the S's! Oh sure, the A to Al was a piece of cake . . . fifty-nine cents each, five thousand of them shouting 'Take me! Take me!' But just try to buy them when they're three ninety-eight and they get a limited number of S's because everyone has dropped out. All the good words are in the S's."

"You should hear yourself," he said. "Is it really that important?"

"Important? Do you want your kids to go through life not knowing the meaning of SEX, the Sabbath, Satire, Scruples, Sin and Status . . . not to mention Sales?"

"The trouble with you," he said, "is you're a pushover for every advertising gimmick that comes down the pike. They could sell you anything."

It was easy for him to say. Men didn't get the pressure from advertising that women did. I'd seen them on the tube. All men ever did was sit around grabbing all the gusto they could get, eating cereal that made them champions, and having a swell time talking to a tub of butter.

When they talked to their broker . . . everyone listened. Even the labels in their shorts danced and had a good time.

Oh, occasionally they'd run a car up the side of a mountain or slap on some after-shave and hit the ports, but mostly it was women who carried the responsibility for the entire family.

And no one cared.

If commercials were supposed to make me feel good about myself, they were failing miserably. My paper towels turned to lace in my hands. My cough medicine ran out at 2 A.M., and my garbage bags broke on impact with the garbage.

It's funny I hadn't thought about it before. I was responsible for my husband's un-derarms being protected for twelve hours. I was responsible for making sure my children had a well-balanced breakfast. I alone was carrying the burden for my dog's shiny coat and spritzing just the right amount of lemon throughout the house so they wouldn't pucker to death. When my daughter's love life fell through it was up to me to remind her that whiter teeth would bring him back.

I was reflecting on my responsibilities when the commercial came on of the husband who came home after a twelve-hour day, beat, depressed and exhausted. He opened the door and seventy-five people jumped up and yelled, "Happy Birthday! Surprise!" The man grabbed his wife, kissed her, and said, "Honey, what a surprise."

She backed off from him like he was a three-day-old dead chicken and said, "What a breath! We'd better do something about it . . . and FAST!"

You would have thought that would have taken the hats and horns out of the occasion if anything would. Instead, we see them in the bathroom, where he is gargling his bad breath into remission. The last scene is one of pure joy. He has finally been allowed to attend his own party and she is beaming, knowing that she has once again saved her husband from himself.

Couldn't the big jerk tell if he had the

breath of a camel? Did his wife have to do everything? I was interrupted by my husband, who came out of the bedroom holding a sport shirt. "Honey," he grinned good-naturedly, "I hate to tell you this, but there's a ring around my collar."

I looked up and snapped, "What a coincidence! It matches the one around your neck!"

I don't know what made me say it . . . only the resentment of being in charge of everyone's welfare, I guess.

I had been naive. I should have realized it the night I showered, put perfume behind each knee, and heard my husband snore in the darkness . . . thus capping the first PG-rated Aviance Night in the history of cosmetics.

I dug out the *Fear of Buying* to find out in what other ways I was being exploited. It was revealing, to say the least. It said grocery shopping is one of the last of the little-known sciences in the world. All the experts know is that it is demanding; it requires great concentration and split-second timing.

For years, researchers have been trying to pin down why women buy as they do, and they have discovered that when a woman enters the store and her hands curl around a cart handle something happens.

Their "eyeblink rate" drops to fourteen a minute, putting them in a hypnoidal trance, which is the first stage of hypnosis. Some of them are even unable to distinguish friends who speak to them.

They cover an aisle in less than twenty seconds, spending on the average of ninety-three cents a minute. Everything in the store has been researched, designed, and color coded to make you buy it. A shopper doesn't stand a chance.

The real stress situation comes at the checkout. Assuming you are able to stave off impulse buying and stick to your list, the real test comes when you unload your groceries on the conveyor belt to be tallied. Here you have candy, gum, magazines, half-price items, special purchases, balloons, breath mints, cigarettes, and fountain pens. Steady now . . . if you can hang on until the bell of the cash register sounds, your blink rate will be up to forty-five a minute and the trance will be broken. You will be able to function once more on a normal level.

Just knowing what was happening to me proved to be of enormous help.

The next time I went to the supermarket I whipped through it like O. J. Simpson making his plane. At the checkout, however, I became uneasy as I saw a line. One woman was shuffling through her handbag trying to find identification for cashing her check.

I tossed a package of razor blades into my basket.

The next woman found a hole in her bag of brown sugar and we waited while the carry-out boy went back to get her a fresh package. I added a kite to my cart.

Two more to go.

The man had a cart full of bottles that

he had been saving since glass was invented. It was his fault I bought the licorice whips.

The lady in front of me only had three items, but the register tape ran out and had to be replaced. Let the patio lights and the birdseed be on her conscience.

Finally it was my turn. The clerk began to tally up my order when she asked, "Do you want that book or are you going to read it here?"

"I'll take it!" I said.

The register bell rang up the total and I came out of my trance. But it was too late. I had a paperback of *Looking for Mr. Goodbody* under my arm.

5

Looking for Mr. Goodbody

The heroines of these books were always the same. A woman, disenchanted, going through life with a nose tissue in one hand and an absorbent towel in the other, decided to go it alone.

She was always tall with "long legs that stretched luxuriously under the sheets."

Her stomach was flat, "belying her three beautiful children."

She had never known ecstasy before.

She had also forgotten about the medical school degree she held until one day when she was lining the knife-and-fork drawer with Contact she ran across it.

She felt guilty about leaving her husband with the three children, $565 a month mortgage payments, a pregnant cat, and a toilet that ran, but "she has to start liking herself" and she can only do that by taking charge of her own life.

At my age, I didn't have the stamina for a rerun. I had begun to note that my body could only do one thing at a time—digest lunch or sit upright.

I wasn't ready to assume the responsibility for the oil changes in my car. I had no curiosity as to where furnace filters went. And besides, I was too domestically geared. (Once when I saw Tom Jones performing in Las Vegas and everyone was throwing their hotel room keys at him, I gave in to an impulse and threw mine. I didn't realize until two days later I had thrown him the key to our freezer.)

Displayed along with the books on married women with a "single" wish were the marriage manuals. They were a trip. I hadn't felt so frustrated since we tried to assemble a bicycle in the closet on Christmas Eve with two washers missing and the instructions written in Japanese.

It made us wonder what we did with our time before Dr. David Reuben invented sex. (One book, *How to Build a Relationship for Pennies in Your Own Home*, even came with an applause sign for over the bed.)

But it was the testimonials to freedom that intrigued me. In a way, I was filled with envy at the heroines . . . especially their zest for living. How my life paled by comparison. All my friends seemed to be moving on to new adventures. A lot of 'em had returned to work . . . some for the money, but most because they needed the rest. Some of my friends were returning to school and the rest of them were redecorating their empty nests with white shag and mirrors.

Me? I was in a holding pattern. None of mine had abandoned the nest and there was no hope in sight.

My daughter thought the red light on the stove was a hidden camera; my son led the life of a hamster; and my other son considered employment a fad like the hula hoop and mood rings.

They were all at the awkward age.

Too old for Dr. Dentons . . . too young for Dr. Scholl's.

Too old for curfews . . . too young for me to go to sleep until they were home.

Too old to advise . . . too young not to need it.

Too old to wash dishes . . . too young to stop eating.

Too old for an income tax exemption . . . too young for Medicare.

I wish I could be like Mayva. She didn't care what her kids did as long as they had clean hands.

It seemed like I had spent a lifetime giving, loving, and sharing. And you know what giving, loving, and sharing got me? It got me a drawer full of dirty pantyhose, a broken stereo, and a wet toothbrush every morning.

It got me a camera with sand in it, a blouse that died from acute perspiration, a sleeping bag with a broken zipper, and a transistor radio that "suddenly went dead, Mom, when it hit the pavement."

Other women my age didn't have kids wandering in and out of their closets like a discount house.

They borrowed my tennis racket, my car, my luggage, and my mouthwash. And my binoculars. I had almost forgotten about my binoculars. When I asked my son what happened to them he said, "They're in my room."

"Well, why don't you put them back where you got them?"

"Why would you want to hang on to a pair of broken binoculars?"

They were driving me crazy with their irregular hours, their slovenly habits, and their lack of responsibility around the house. Besides, they had reached the point where they had learned all of my adult expressions and were using them on me.

"Are you going to clean your room today?" I asked.

"We'll see."

"It worries me when you're out until all hours of the morning."

"Big people should not worry about little people. We can take care of ourselves."

"Well, I don't like it and I'm not going to put up with it."

"Don't use that tone. You're just tired and crabby. Why don't you take a little nap and we'll talk about it when you wake up."

I had visions of my being the oldest living mother in North America with children at home. I'd be ninety-five and my daughter would be borrowing my last clean pair of SuppHose, my sons installing an automatic Genie door on the refrigerator . . . and every Mother's Day having them chip in and buy me another tooth.

Wanda would have handled it differently. Wanda was the heroine in the book I was reading, *Wanda's Cry of May Day.* What a woman! One day she just marched out of a pillowcase bingo game and into a singles salad bar, where she ordered a spinach salad with bacon bits. Within three minutes she had struck up a relationship with a man with a tossed salad, bean sprouts, and Thousand Island dressing. She slept with him before their salads digested.

The next day she got a job as vice president of a TV network and threw herself into her work. But she couldn't forget the tossed-salad-with-bean-sprouts-and-Thousand-Island-dressing encounter.

She tried. She produced a documentary in Greece, a miniseries in Russia, and got her Ph.D. at nights. TS with BS and TI called her every day, but she knew what she wanted.

Less than ninety-six pages later she married him, settled down, and on the last page was playing pillowcase bingo and for the first time in a long time felt good about herself.

My husband and I were at the beach when I finished the last chapter. I looked down. I had buried my varicose veins beneath the sand. The flies were going crazy over my hair spray.

My husband was sitting next to me swathed in beach towels to avoid the sun, balancing the checkbook.

It wasn't exactly the surf-and-sand scene in *From Here to Eternity*.

Okay, so I was content to live vicariously through Wanda and all the others, but was it wrong to want to shift to the next plateau of my life? I approached my daughter with the problem.

"I don't know how to tell you this, but you are keeping me from shifting gears and going on to the next phase of my wonderfulness. Another year or so and it may be too late."

"What are you trying to say?"

"I guess what I'm trying to say is there are a lot of colleges away from home that provide an opportunity for a person to mingle with people from all kinds of different and exciting backgrounds. In an atmosphere of this sort, there is room to grow and to mature. Isolation from family usually forces one to take charge of one's own life, make one's own priorities, and carry them out without interference. Do you know what I am trying to say?"

She put her hand on mine, "If you wanted to go away to school, Mom, why didn't you say so? We'll manage. We'll eat out a lot."

"You don't understand," I said, biting my lip. "Life is divided into many cycles. We have an infant cycle, a childhood cycle, a teenage cycle, a married cycle, and the Grape-Nuts cycle. The end of each cycle is a little frightening because it means change and change means adjusting, but one has to move on, do you understand?"

She nodded and I felt reassured.

"It's a big decision to enter into the next cycle, but if one keeps in mind there are friends who are supportive, striking out on your own isn't bad."

"If you and Dad wanted your own apartment," she said, "why didn't you say so? We never dreamt we were getting in your way. This house has to be a lot for you.

What you're saying is right. If you feel like you want to come back from time to time, we'll all still be here."

I was locked in forever with a counter-top of dirty glasses, nose tissue left in jeans pockets, and corn pads that patched the water beds.

"You should be putting your own life together," I said, making one last stab at it. "You have to learn that clean pantyhose do not perpetuate themselves and the meaning of life is more than an herbal connection. If you go away to school you will be responsi-ble for yourself. You'll find self-reliance, in-dependence, feet! Yes, feet. There's a whole group of people out there you've never met before. They're called pedestrians."

"You are saying you want me to bug off? Split?"

"I wouldn't have phrased it that way."

"Am I getting close?"

"Your father and I love you, but it's time to move on."

"I understand," she said. "After this semester ends, I'll start shopping around for a college farther away from home."

Why was it every time I did something that was good for the kids, I felt rotten?

While in the library returning *Wendy's Pool Table Fetish and Other Fantasies* I met my friend Nancy.

We talked about my holding pattern and the exodus of my firstborn, then she smiled and said, "It should be apparent what is wrong with you. You're going through your midlife crisis."

"It sounds redundant," I said.

"Believe me," said Nancy, "I know where you're coming from. You feel used up, unfulfilled, unappreciated. Your life is in the Twilight Zone. And you live in fear. Fear that your children are writing a sequel to *Mommie Dearest*. Fear of dying after you've just eaten a crummy, tasteless salad with a low-calorie dressing. Fear of going to a partner-swapping party and no one wants to swap with you."

"That's not true," I said. "I may complain but I have a fulfilling life."

"I've seen your social calendar," said Nancy. "It looks like it belongs to a shut-in. Have you never awakened in the morning, looked into a mirror, and said aloud, 'I am never going to be Ambassador to Uganda. My legs will never fit into a boot without a zipper. I will never successfully grow a Boston fern or win the *Reader's Digest* Sweepstakes. I am built like a caftan'?"

"Nancy," I said. "Whatever I am, I do not talk to myself. And I do not live in fear of anything. I am a perfectly well-adjusted person."

"Look," she said, "I've got a book that not only tells you what crisis is going to appear next in your life, it tells you how to deal with it. It's called *Packages* and each chapter deals with one little bundle after another of what is in store for you as you reach a certain age. It's like seeing your future before it gets here."

I didn't think about Nancy or the book until a few days later. As I brushed my teeth, I looked into my reflection in the mirror and for no apparent reason said out loud, "Breathes there a woman with soul so dead/Who never to herself hath said . . . My God! I'm talking to myself."

I went to the library and checked out *Packages* by Gayle Teehee.

6

Is There Life after Packages?

If there's anything my life had been, it had been predictable. You could set your clock by it. Acne at twelve, marriage at twenty-two, labor pains at twenty-six, Miss Clairol at thirty, Sara Lee at thirty-five, and turtleneck sweaters at forty.

I certainly didn't need a book to tell me the twenties had been traumatic, the thirties illusion-shattering, the forties restless and the fifties . . . my God, only two pages titled "Resignation" jammed between turtleneck sweaters and the index.

Packages didn't waste words. (I guess

they figured there wasn't time to waste.) They said I was living in an age of fear. Fear of unfulfillment. Fear of what people thought of me. Fear of poor health. Fear of old age.

That wasn't true. I didn't fear old age. I was just becoming increasingly aware of the fact that the only people who said old age was beautiful were usually twenty-three years old.

In my heart I just refused to believe that Shirley Temple Black was toilet-trained. Oh, there were a few moments of sensitivity. On a trip to renew my driver's license the man behind the counter asked the date of my birth in a loud voice. They tell me I slammed him against the wall, locked my forearm against his throat, and shouted, "Let us just say I'm somewhere between estrogen and death!"

Packages said I had a fear of not knowing what life held for me . . . fear of being abandoned . . . fear of being alone. Were they kidding? As a woman who once named the NFL in an alienation suit, I wrote the book on loneliness. When someone cloned Howard Cosell, I'd begin to worry.

Fear of loss of interest in sex (that was scarcely a problem to a couple who viewed an R-rated movie for the plot) and a fear of phobias.

I slammed the book shut. It was obvious. I was late for my crisis and it had started without me. Why, I didn't have a phobia in the world.

I was feeling rather pleased with myself when my daughter bounded into the house, threw her car keys on the table, and said, "Guess who's pregnant?"

"Give me a hint."

"Bunny's mother, Barfy."

"Get serious," I laughed. "Barfy is a year older than I am and two years younger than Mickey Mouse."

"Tell her. She thinks she's Bugs Bunny. I think it's neat. How come you don't have another baby? In a few years we'll all be gone. What will you do to replace us?"

"I'll get measles."

"A lot of my girlfriends' mothers are

getting pregnant. They say having babies makes you feel ten years younger."

"Than what? And what girlfriends' mothers? Name names!"

"There's Wheezie's mother, Wizard. Cooky's mother, Corky, and possibly Holly's mother, Berry."

When she was gone, I slumped dejectedly into a chair. I had never been so depressed in my life. What was happening? I had an antique quilt younger than Berry. So there was one fear of midlife I hadn't counted on—Guinnessaphobia: the fear of having a baby after forty.

I couldn't do it. I didn't care what they said about caboose children being such a bonus. If it happened, I'd adjust, but under anesthesia I'd deny I ever said it.

I was too tired for a new family. I fell asleep having my teeth cleaned. I dozed at parties that dragged on until ten o'clock. I couldn't cross my legs after a big meal. One 2 A.M. feeding and I'd have bags under my eyes that would take surgery to correct.

My intellect was dulled. I didn't know

any more why God wasn't married, what the inside of a volleyball looked like, or how come my biscuit dough never laughed when you punched it.

I had been there. There were no surprises. I'd spent three rainy days with three kids with chickenpox with a broken washer. I'd fainted from blowing up swimming pools. I'd traveled through three states with a bag of wet diapers under the seat and two kids in the back arguing over a piece of gum with lint on it.

I'd wrestled with strollers on escalators, fights with holy water, and hysteria on the first day of school.

A few days later I saw Barfy in the supermarket. She had that pregnant stance, like a kangaroo wearing earth shoes. She looked tired.

"Barfy!" I said solicitously, staring at her stomach. "What happened?"

"Would you believe I'm carrying it for a friend?"

"I'm sorry," I said. "It was just such a shock."

"It's okay. I get a lot of dumb questions. Like 'Good heavens, are you still walking around with that baby?'"

"I thought you were on the pill."

"We all were. Wizard, Corky, and Berry. There are no guarantees, you know. Every day someone is suing the pharmaceutical companies."

"No guarantees," I said numbly. "I'll bet your family was surprised."

"They're ecstatic," she said. "They can hardly wait until it gets here. There are all kinds of promises to change it, feed it, and play with it, but I'm afraid it'll be like Winnie's baby. You remember Winnie. Her kids promised her she wouldn't have to raise an arthritic finger after the baby was born. She was suspicious, but at age forty-three, she finally gave in. When the baby was born she called her daughter to look at it. 'Well,' said Winnie, 'What do you think of your new responsibility?' Her daughter looked at the baby, shrugged and said, 'I changed my mind. I'd rather have a new Bee Gees album.'"

"Gosh, Barfy, isn't it weird being in the doctor's waiting room with all the young girls?"

"Sure, but things have changed nowadays since we had our babies. They breathe them out now. Everything is natural and your husband is with you throughout the birth. Remember how it used to be?"

"Do I ever! I became hysterical and frightened and begged for sedation. And that was just the first prenatal visit."

"It's a whole new ballgame," sighed Barfy. "Super-absorbent throwaways, shoulder slings to carry them around, no bottles to fiddle with, and a new relaxed atmosphere."

"I'm sorry, Barfy, but I can't imagine a delivery without a hairdresser in attendance. That is just too primitive for me."

That night I had trouble sleeping. All kinds of pictures flashed before my eyes . . . swallowing a diaper pin at age sixty-five, having my baby push me around in a stroller at the zoo, napping during delivery, receiving a pacemaker for Mother's Day, fighting the kid for the baby food, spanking my toddler for coloring on my Social Security check, becoming the first Medicare subscriber to put in a claim for delivery.

The fact was I didn't want to look my age, but I didn't want to act the age I wanted to look either. I also wanted to grow old enough to understand that sentence.

There was definitely a youth cult in this country where people worshiped at the shrine of taut skin and shiny hair. Where only concave stomachs made the billboards and second young wives were royalty.

If you had a wrinkle, you took a snip.

If something sagged, you took a tuck.

If it jiggled, firm it up.

If it stuck out, suck it in.

If it was gray, touch it up.

New faces began to emerge among my old friends. Faces that looked like masks. In fact, I had seen more wrinkles on a baby's bottom. I remember how excited I got one day when I discovered a cosmetic stick that would erase away the lines. I erased my entire face.

According to *Packages* you were supposed to have a no-panic approach to physical aging, but it wasn't easy when all around you emphasis was put on how old you looked.

I didn't face up to my age until one afternoon when I was lying on the sofa half asleep, half absorbed in the old movie *Sunset Boulevard*, starring Gloria Swanson and Bill Holden. I had seen it a dozen times, but loved it. It was the big scene. The one where Bill Holden is leaving the aging movie star, Norma Desmond. A line in his speech nearly brought me off the sofa. He said, "There's nothing tragic about being fifty, Norma, unless you're trying to look like twenty-five."

FIFTY! NORMA DESMOND HAD BEEN FIFTY ALL THOSE YEARS? I had remembered her as ninety-seven if she was a day.

I watched in horror as she descended the staircase, the camera grinding away, the lights on her face. She was only a baby.

I turned on the bathroom light and scrutinized myself carefully. One was always led to believe that aging was a gradual process. It just wasn't true. I went to bed one night and in the morning was struck with all the diseases of the decade I had to live through for the next ten years.

Overnight, I developed a case of LOSS OF MENU. At first I blamed candle failure. Then small print. When I had to drop the menu on the floor to see it or ask the waiter to back into a far wall until I focused, it became apparent I needed glasses.

The next to strike was REUNION ANXIETY. I had dreaded it for years, but no one could have prepared me for the moment I arrived at my reunion and one after another said, "You look fantastic!"

Everyone knows when you are twenty, the greeting is "How are you?," and when you're thirty it's "What are you up to these days?" But when you're over the hill, the standard greeting is "You look fantastic!" Sometimes it's accompanied by the word

"Really!," which is supposed to offer you reassurance.

PREMATURE NOSTALGIA was predictable. Day by day I watched my high school years being satirized in TV sitcoms. My clothing came back into style and the music of my youth was being imitated and satirized. For a while I tried looking blank when someone mentioned Patti Page, but it fooled no one.

The HAVE I TAKEN MY PILL YET FETISH was the hardest to adjust to. One morning I looked at the window ledge over the sink and there was a line of pills to keep me operational. They never seemed to make any difference, they were just there . . . little bottles of pills with childproof caps. Despite them I still suffered from leg cramps all night when I wore heels to a party.

My case of MEMORY DEFICIENCY became a classic. I got on a salt kick. One week I ran out of salt and made a mental note to buy it. For every week after that for about two years, I bought a box of salt because I couldn't remember if I had bought it originally. Every time I tried to remember the age of my middle child, I had to go back to the year of his birth and count up. Memory deficiency got so bad with me, I forgot to repeat a piece of gossip I swore on my Grandmother's Grave never to divulge.

But the worst disease of my midlife was a case of INSUBORDINATE BODY. In my youth, my brain would say to my feet, "Take that laundry to the second floor." NOT ANY MORE. The legs rebelled and I stacked so many things at the bottom of the stairs I nearly killed myself.

I must have read the chapter on Resignation a hundred times and each time became more depressed. It sounded like I was approaching the prime of my senility.

We were going into the middle of July when my daughter announced she was going away to school in the northern part of the state. She was happy about it.

I confided to my hairdresser, Mr. Steve, about her decision: "Isn't that just like children? You devote your life to them . . . spoon-feed them, sit with them all night under a vaporizer, pack them with vitamins, straighten their teeth, curl their hair, care for them, love them, and they reach twenty or so and pick up and leave you."

"I thought that's what you wanted," he said.

"It's not what I wanted. It's what comes with my midlife cycle. Don't you understand? My life is all arranged for me. At a certain age we must shift gears and go on to the next phase of our life. I have no control over it."

"Of course you have control over your life," he said, swinging me around in my chair. "Tell me, what sign were you born under?"

I shrugged. "My birthday is February twenty-first."

"Umm, I thought so," he said. "Pisces. That explains everything. Forget all this mishmash about your life being predictable. I tell you you can control your own destiny if you just heed your sign. I swear by a book called *Get Off Your Cusp and Live!* by Jeanne Vixon. The moment I looked at you, I knew your moon was in her second decan, which added a secret longing to your Neptunian impregnability, and that the latter decan is augmented by tempestuous Mars, which offers energy and immeasurable support."

"What does that mean?"

"Either you start using moisturizer around your eyes, sweetie, or lay in a supply of wood filler!"

7

Get Off
Your Cusp and Live!

Ever since I read that Eva Braun (Hitler's mistress), Judas Iscariot, and Anne Boleyn shared my zodiac sign, I could never get too choked up about Astrology.

Mr. Steve meant well, but he didn't know what a loser I was. My sun never rose on my sign. My planets were always conspiring behind my back. And my destiny always read like it had been out in the natal sun too long.

Maybe I was just bitter, but it always seemed like other people got the good signs. Their horoscopes always read "Popularity and untold wealth will haunt you. There is no getting away from it. You are irresistible to every sign in the zodiac. Give in and enjoy."

Not mine. It was always an ominous warning like "Watch your purse." "Your high school acne was only in remission, and will return the fifteenth of the month." "Don't become discouraged by your friends who will take advantage of you."

Somehow, I always felt if Mother had held on a little longer—a good month and a half—things would have been different for me.

Oh, I had faith in the predictions. It was just that my interpretation of my sign was not always the way it turned out. For example:

Prediction: "You get a chance today to provide guidance and inspiration."

Fact: I chaperoned thirty fourth-graders on a tour of a meat-packing plant.

Prediction: "One you thought had abandoned you is back in the picture."

Fact: We found a roach under the sink.

Prediction: "Married or single, this is a 'power' time for you!"

Fact: The heat went off for four hours.

Prediction: "You have a unique way of expressing yourself, and you could gain much satisfaction by writing."

Fact: I wrote a check to have the septic tank cleaned.

Mr. Steve didn't tell me that keeping up with my stars was a full-time job. The daily forecast in the paper was brief and scanty. I had to buy a magazine to find out my food forecast, one for my sex forecast, one for my fashion predictions, another for my travel, and still another for my decoration sense, color selection, and perfume.

I wanted to clean out my refrigerator one day but didn't dare because my sign said avoid the color green.

I canceled trips, put off foot surgery, didn't invite Virgos to my party, and on the advice of my horoscope did not handle money for an entire month. (If it hadn't been for my charge card, I'd have died.) There was so much to learn about myself. I was absolutely fascinating. I discovered women born under my sign were dynamic, confident, and into asparagus. I was an orange person, trusting, French provincial with boundless energy, and long-waisted.

One evening at a jewelry party, one of the brownies I was serving dropped on the carpet. I reached over, picked it off the floor, popped it in my mouth, and said, "A fuzzy brownie never hurt anyone."

A woman I knew only as Nicky looked deep into my eyes and nodded knowingly. "Only a Pisces on the cusp would say that."

I asked her how she knew. She said certain traits belonged to certain signs. According to my birth date, I was born on a rising sign which made my destiny special. I was a wonderful homemaker, excellent cook, and fine seamstress. That wasn't a destiny. It was a sentence!

There had to be something wrong.

What happened to dynamic, confident, and asparagus?

"You're on the rise," she said, "and the sun and the moon are in the direct line with the tides."

I felt like my tide had just gone out.

A cook?

Everyone knew I always threatened my children with "If you don't shape up, you go to bed *with* dinner."

A homemaker?

I wanted for Christmas what Phyllis Diller always wanted . . . an oven that flushed.

A seamstress?

I always considered a fallen button as God's way of telling us the shirt was wrong.

"You're born under a wonderful sign," Nicky gushed. "You are gentle and expect to have the least and the last. You end up with the bent fork, but you never complain. You buy a three-piece weekender outfit with a skirt and a pair of slacks and burn a hole in the jacket, but you don't care. You always come out of the rest room dragging a piece of toilet tissue on your shoe, but you don't mind."

"Why don't I mind?" I asked.

"Because it's your nature. Why I know of one woman born under your natal sign who had a son at camp. On parents' visitation day, she had flu and was seven months pregnant, but she drove the two hundred miles along a dusty road. She had a flat tire and lost her way twice. But she kept going. She made it to the camp and when all the boys were introducing their parents, her son—who was going through a difficult time of his life relating to parents—said, 'My Mom couldn't come.' Do you know what she did?"

"She killed him," I said hopefully.

"She just shrugged and said, 'I could have predicted it because my sun is on the rise and I am on the cusp.' My dear, people under your sign inherit the earth."

I didn't want the earth. I wanted dynamic. Instead, I had fallen heir to the Klutzism Sign. Stumbling around life fifty-two weeks out of every year rubbing stains off my sweater, putting the wrong dates on checks, and never being able to trust myself to run the course in Better China with a shoulder bag.

What kind of a future did I have to look forward to? I locked all the doors in the car and left the top down. Broke my tooth on a marshmallow and got sucked up in my son's hair dryer and sprained my shoulder.

I liked me better when I didn't know who I was, what I was, or where I was going. Besides, my daughter had gone off to school taking with her all the small appliances, furniture, linens, bedding, TV set, typewriter, and staples.

My husband noticed it right away. "You let her pack off everything we've worked thirty years to accumulate?"

I shrugged. "What can I tell you? My sun is on the rise."

I found myself spending more time in the kitchen. Maybe I was creative and there was something in my personality I had overlooked. I bought a food processor and shredded myself to death. I bought a microwave oven and stood by helplessly while my son's space maintainer turned to liquid when he left it in a sandwich I was reheating. I got out of the kitchen before I hurt myself.

I bought a sewing machine that did everything but answer the door, and decided to make a jacket. The darts faced the wrong way, the buttonholes were ahead of their time (no button had been manufactured for it yet). The lining grew each evening as I slept. It had been laundered three times and never been worn.

In stitching up new curtains one afternoon for my daughter's vacated bedroom, a book fell to the floor. It was called *Far Out and Far East* by Edith Marishna. On the cover was a picture of a woman sitting cross-legged, her turban-covered head tilted backward, staring toward the sky.

I knew my daughter was fascinated with Transcendental Meditation. In fact, she had even taken me to the Golden Temple of Zucchini one day for lunch. It was one of those pure-food restaurants near the local college campus where everything was either freshly squeezed or grown before your eyes. We ordered the organic bean sprouts jammed between two hydroponic tomatoes. "I think I'm going to go crazy and order a cranberry malt," I said.

A man with a turban appeared at our table and elevated the malt over his head as if it were a chalice. I felt positively sanctified until I discovered my lunch contained 1200 calories.

I had never meditated. Oh, once when I paid thirty dollars for a Halston scarf I slipped into a slight hypnotic state. But I had never meditated like the girl on the cover. The book jacket said everyone needed to create an organically oriented womb of tranquility in which to grow spiritually and pull your life together. It said I could have inner peace by controlling my own destiny. It was in my hands. I could be in control of myself by taking a few minutes out of each day and reciting a special word over and over again. The word was called a mantra.

At dinner that night my husband's fork

poised over a bowl of green slime. "What's this?" he asked.

"It's puréed lettuce. I put the wrong setting on the food processor. It's easier if you eat it with a spoon."

"Do you have any idea how long it has been since we have eaten anything whole? I never see whole food any more. If I am not going to see whole food, the least you can do is to label it. Isn't there a federal law that you have to label what you are eating?"

"You don't have to shout."

"Someone should shout around here. Patterns all over the table every night, needles everywhere. Appliances whirring day and night. Weird things growing restless in the refrigerator. It's driving me crazy."

As I sat there listening to him rant, a thought occurred to me. He wasn't meek. He wasn't gentle. He wasn't resigned to pain. He certainly wasn't domestic and didn't have a long waist. AND OUR BIRTHDAY WAS ONLY TWO DAYS APART. WE WERE BORN UNDER THE SAME SIGN!

On my way to bed I picked up *Far Out*

and Far East and turned on the bedside light.

It was time to get off my cusp and start controlling my own life. I was going to have inner peace if I had to break a few heads to do it.

8

Raising Consciousness in Your Own Home for Fun and Profit

For years, I have studied the phenomenon of the mother who sits down for a moment to get off her feet. From all I've been able to gather, a message goes out over an invisible network that flashes to the world "Mother is in a sitting position. Proceed and de-sit."

At that moment the doorbell will ring, children will appear holding vital parts of their anatomy, the dog will dig his paws insistently into a leg, a husband will call impatiently for help, a phone will register its fifteenth ring, a pot will boil over, a buzzer will sound, or faucets will go on all over the house, and a loud voice will shriek, "I'm telling."

The "Mother is sitting" phenomenon is probably one of the reasons meditation never really got a foothold on mothers when they were the ones who needed it the most.

All I know is I was possibly the only woman in the world dedicated to inner peace and tranquility who would end up with varicose veins of the neck from shouting.

"Tranquility" also presented another problem. It said I would need a mantra . . . a word that when repeated over and over again would transport me to a level of calmness and give me untold energy.

I called my daughter at school. "Did you get a mantra with *Far Out and Far East?*"

"Of course I didn't get a mantra. Even if I did, I couldn't let you use it. Each one is personal and given only to that person. They're secret. You have to buy them."

"How much do they cost?" I asked.

"It depends. Sometimes a couple hundred dollars."

I had no intention of paying more for a word than I paid for our first car. In discussing this one day at the supermarket with Natalie, a friend, she said she had a mantra that had barely been used. She told me she had only chanted it for three months prior to her divorce and would let it go for $12.50.

"What's wrong with it?" I asked suspiciously.

"Nothing. It's just that I couldn't do housework with my legs permanently folded. Trust me, it works. Whenever you come face to face with a situation that makes you tense, just sit down wherever you are, cross your legs, turn your palms to the ceiling, and recite your mantra over and over again."

The next day I went into my son's bedroom and was knocked against the wall by an odor. It took twenty minutes to track it down, but I finally found it. Under a stack of clothes on the chair was a doggy bag holding a chicken leg and a breast he brought home from his birthday dinner. His birthday was celebrated two weeks ago.

I felt like a fool, but I sat cross-legged in his bed, turned my palms toward the ceiling, and began to mumble my word. When the washer buzzer went off, instead of running out to get the softener in before the final rinse, I kept repeating my word.

Afterward, I felt rather refreshed and for the first time in a long time sat down to a full breakfast of orange juice, French toast, and coffee.

Later in the morning, I discovered one of the kids had left the phone off the hook. Instead of biting the phone cord in half, I just sat cross-legged in the middle of the floor, meditated, and had a cookie and a glass of milk.

That afternoon when I went to get into the car and discovered someone had left my car door open and the light had run my battery down, I squatted, recited my mantra, and was revitalized again. My newfound calm was rewarded with a piece of banana cake. When my husband came home I was eating a bowl of potato chips and drinking a diet cola.

"Aren't you pigging out a little more than usual?"

"Oh, c'mon," I said. "Maybe I have been a little more relaxed than usual but . . ."

"If you get any more relaxed, you won't be able to fit through a door."

"I don't care what you say. I've got my peace of mind."

"It's probably the only thing you can get into."

"That is all you know. How many women do you know who can still slip into the clothes they wore when they were newly married?" (It was true. Just that morning, I got into my maternity underwear and they slipped right over my hips.)

Even the boys began to notice that I was growing again. The combination of staying in the house, being alone so much, and being relaxed had turned me into an inflatable.

One afternoon when my son came bounding into the house he said, "Sorry, Mom, I didn't know you were meditating."

"I'm not."

"Then why are you sitting cross-legged on the couch?"

"I'm not sitting cross-legged. Those are my hips."

That night when I stepped out of the shower, I looked into the mirror. The soufflé of my youth had fallen. Edith Marishna and her energy. As I sat in my lotus position, I was struck by a brutal truth. It would take an Act of God to get me to my feet.

It was discouraging. Just as soon as I got my head together, my body went. It wasn't fair. All my life I had dieted. I was bored talking about it . . . bored thinking about it—and tired of planning my next meal.

As I sat there sucking in my stomach and seeing nothing move, the twelfth major religion of the world began to form in my mind.

A religion founded in the twentieth century based on the four ignoble truths:

BLOUSES WORN OUTSIDE THE
SLACKS FOOL NO ONE.
ONE-SIZE-FITS-ALL IS AN IN-
COMPLETE SENTENCE.
IF THERE'S LIFE AFTER
WHIPPED CREAM, IT'S IN
THIGH CITY.
STARCHING A CAFTAN NEVER
SOLVES ANYTHING.

I would call my new religion FATSU. The disciples would be every woman who has ever gone to bed hungry and who sought a destiny of pantyhose that bagged at the knee.

The day of worship would be Monday, what else?

And the daily chant would be MaryTylerMoore . . . MaryTylerMoore . . . MaryTylerMoore . . .

I could almost see Jean Nieditch standing in the middle of thunder and lightning while the seven FATSU commandments were being flashed on a head of lettuce:

THOU SHALT NOT PUNISH THYSELF BY TRYING ON A BATHING SUIT WEARING KNEE HI'S.

THOU SHALT NOT CONSIDER GRAVY AND HOLLANDAISE SAUCE A BEVERAGE.

THOU SHALT NOT KILL FOR CHOCOLATE.

THOU SHALT NOT STEAL HALLOWEEN CANDY FROM THY CHILDREN.

THOU SHALT HAVE NO OTHER MIRRORS BEFORE THEE BUT MY SPECIAL ONES.

THOU SHALT NOT TAKE THE NAME OF COTTAGE CHEESE IN VAIN.

THOU SHALT NOT COVET THY NEIGHBOR'S DESSERT.

Banded together, we would surpass the Shinto, Confucian, Hindu, and even the Moslem religions in numbers. Our disciples would roam the earth spreading the word:

starvation. Maybe once a year we'd have a sacrifice by throwing a butterscotch sundae off a cliff. On that day we'd all fast, of course.

We'd separate our beliefs from the state, interfering only when they tried to take away artificial sweeteners.

My followers were immortalizing me in two panels of stained glass (with a wide load on them) when my husband interrupted my meditation and brought me back to reality.

"How much do you weigh now?"

I stiffened. "There are three things you never ask a woman: her age, her weight, and the date on the newspapers lining her kitchen cupboards."

"You really have spread out in the past few months. If you ask me you're spending entirely too much time sitting around the house chanting and eating. You should get out more . . . and get some exercise."

I knew it. I wondered when he'd get around to his pitch on jogging. If there is anything more sanctimonious than a man who has been jogging for eight years I don't know what it is. He wouldn't be happy until he got the entire family running around in the darkness being chased by vicious dogs and unmarked cars. Joggers were all alike, running by the house every morning like a Fruit of the Loom pageant. In all the months they huffed and puffed by the house, four abreast, drenched in their own sweat, their chests heaving in and out, I had never once seen one of them smile.

No, if I were going to lose weight, I'd do it my own way. Evelyn had a new diet she was talking about at card club. It was supposed to be a real breakthrough for dieters. I think she called it "Is Something Eating You? Or Vice Versa." After all, Evelyn was a professional dieter. There wasn't one she hadn't tried. During her lifetime she had lost 3,476 pounds. Most of in her neck and bust.

In her kitchen was an entire bookshelf of captivating titles . . . all current best sellers. There were:

The Neurosis Cookbook. You never outgrow your need for paranoia. Two hundred pages of new, low-calorie meals for encounter-group picnics and postnatal-depression snacks.

Did You Ever See a Fat Gerbil? This was a provocative title on how sex could make you thin by burning up 31,955 calories a year. By kissing three times a day (at nine calories each) and engaging in two amorous interludes a week (at 212 calories) you could (if you excuse the expression) conceivably lose 9.13 pounds a year.

The Mexican Quick Loss Program was relatively simple to follow. You traveled to Mexico, drank a glass of water, and ate a head of lettuce. Wear gym shoes.

There were scores more, from Dr. Witherall's flavored ice diet to *How to Face a Visit from Your Mother on 1200 Calories a Day.*

I picked up *Is Something Eating You? Or Vice Versa.* "Does this diet really work?" I asked Evelyn.

She wrinkled her brow. "Is that the one by Dr. Barnhiser where when you get so hungry you can't stand it, you get in the car and drive around until you hit something?"

"I don't think so," I said. "It's the one where your emotions dictate what you eat."

"I remember," she said. "I lost five pounds and three friends on that one. Listen, if you're really serious about losing weight, why don't you go to the LUMP meetings?"

"LUMP?" I said slowly.

"It stands for Lose by Unappetizing Meals and Pressure."

"Is it a group therapy thing?"

"You got it," said Evelyn. "Once a week you go to a public meeting where you fall on your knees in front of the group and confess your caloric sins. The leader is either filled with disgust at the sight of you or rewards you with a liver malt. If you have gained, you must carry a bowling ball around for a week."

"That sounds reasonable," I said. "Maybe I'll go."

The El Gordo chapter of LUMP met once a week within a few blocks of me. I introduced myself to a group of members who were in the hallway popping water pills and removing their jewelry before they weighed in.

Following an X-rated movie—*The Birth of an Éclair*—our leader, Frances, launched into a discussion of the much-maligned staple of the LUMP diet . . . liver.

"In order for the diet to work," she said, "everyone has to consume at least sixteen ounces of liver a week." She didn't care how we disguised it.

Early in my life I had made a pact with myself. I would never eat anything that moved when I cooked it, excited the dog, or inflated upon impact with my teeth.

I didn't mind starving with LUMP's diet, but couldn't bring myself to eat anything that, when dropped on the floor, you found yourself apologizing to.

I was in LUMP's program three weeks, during which time I did everything with liver but put a dress on it. It didn't work.

Besides, I had only lost a pound and a half—which I attributed to my less frequent trips to the refrigerator (which were slowed down when I dropped the bowling ball on my foot).

The solution to losing weight was obvious to me. I'd have to stop meditating. It was too bad, because I really enjoyed sitting cross-legged in the middle of a tense situation in open defiance of bells, buzzers, screams, threats, and the secret society to get mothers on their feet.

It was with deep regret that I called my friend, Donna, to see if she wanted to buy my mantra for $8.50.

As I left Donna, she was sitting cross-legged on the floor, her palms toward the ceiling, her head tilted to the sky, chanting "PAULNEWMANPAULNEWMANPAULNEW-MANPAULNEW . . ."

I left quickly before I changed my mind.

9

The Complete Book of Jogging

Jim Fixit's legs were the first thing I saw every morning and the last thing I saw every night.

They were on the cover of his best seller, *The Complete Book of Jogging*. For the past two years my husband had followed the gospel according to St. James Fixit. He ate Jim's cereal, took Jim's warming-up exercises, adopted Jim's form, ran with Jim in races whenever he could, and occasionally—when he thought no one was looking—lived out his fantasy by posing his legs in front of the mirror like the legs on the cover of the book.

When he wasn't poring over the pages of the book, it was on the nightstand by our bed next to the liniment.

My husband knew how I felt about physical fitness. I hated skiing or any other sport where there was an ambulance waiting at the bottom of the hill. As a golfer with a slice, I found the game lonely. And it became apparent to me long ago that if God had wanted me to play tennis, He would have given me less leg and more room to store the ball.

Despite this, I knew it was only a matter of time before he pointed out that my inner peace had brought me outer fat and tried to convert me to jogging.

Joggers were like that. In no other sport were the participants so evangelistic. They talked of nothing else.

The children of runners would huddle in groups and whisper: "Who told you about jogging? Your mother or your father? Or did you learn about it in the gutter?"

Whenever a group of four would gather, someone would open the conversation with "Where were you and what were you doing when you heard that Bill Rogers won the Boston Marathon? I remember I was washing my hair when the bulletin came over the news."

One night I was dancing with one of my husband's friends when he whispered, "Sure, I could go jogging with you this weekend, but would you respect me in the morning?"

They bragged about their blisters, their Achilles tendonitis, their chondromalacia of the knee, their foot bursitis, shin splints, pulled leg muscles, back pains, and muscle cramps. Their stories made you sick you missed World War II.

I watched the joggers every morning from my kitchen window. They looked like an organized death march as they ran by gasping, perspiring, stumbling, their faces contorted with pain. I never had the urge to "cut in."

One night as I crawled into bed, I inadvertently set my root beer float on top of

Jim Fixit's book. Horrified, my husband grabbed the book and wiped the jacket off with the sleeve of his pajama. "What kind of an animal are you?"

I thought then he might launch into his sanctimonious how-good-you'd-feel-if-you-got-up-at-five-thirty-and-ran-ten-miles speech, but he didn't.

I continued to reward my frustrations with food and he continued to run every day and brag about his jogger's elbow (which he got when he sideswiped a stop sign at an intersection). One morning when he returned from his run he asked brightly, "Guess who I saw running in the park?"

Before I could answer he said, "Louise Cremshaw. Remember her?"

Louise Cremshaw! We used to follow her around for shade. "Of course I remember Louise," I said. "She was the only girl in our class who had to have the sleeves let out in her graduation gown."

"Not any more," he said, grabbing for a box of Jim Fixit's cereal. "She's been running and she's a real knockout."

That did it. "Okay," I said, throwing down the dish towel. "You've won. You've penetrated the barrier of good sense. I am yours. I will start to jog. Just tell me which chapters to start reading in *The Complete Book of Jogging*."

"There are a lot of books you can read," he hedged. "There's *Inner Walking* by Tad Victor. He's the guy who wrote *Inner Bowling*, *Inner Roller Skating*, and *Inner Gooney Golf*."

"What's wrong with my reading your *Complete Book of Jogging*?"

"Wait until you're serious about it. Besides, you have to learn to walk before you can jog."

Inner Walking said there were two people within my body (I certainly had the stomach for it). The outer part of me was instinctively competitive. But the inner part of me needed work. I had to teach myself to concentrate and to remove self-doubts about myself and my abilities.

It said a lot of sports people used the inner theory that said within you there is a better you than you think there is. I read about the skiers who subscribed to this theory and didn't regard bumps as adversaries, but as friends. They would ski over each one saying, "Thank you, bump."

Or bowlers who threw a gutter ball would say, "Thank you, gutter, for being there." Or the gooney golf players who didn't always make the cup but were grateful that the ball didn't land in the middle of the expressway. What they were really saying is that I had to be psyched up for walking and not be discouraged.

When a boulder lodged in my shoe, I said, "Thank you, rock, for nearly severing my toe from my foot."

When a car with a bumper sticker that read "I found it" nearly ran me off the road, I said, "Thank you, car, for not strapping me to your hood to show everyone what you found today."

As I ran into the driveway, my husband said, "I thought you were supposed to be walking."

"I was," I panted, "until I ran out of Twinkies to hold off the dogs."

He said I was ready for Jim Fixit's book.

That night he brought it to the dining-room table and gently placed it before me like a chalice. In keeping with the moment, I genuflected and said a little prayer.

The big thing about jogging was that it was a pure sport. It was just you in a little pair of raggy gym shoes, a pair of shorts, and your own patch of lonely road. That was beautiful. Like a Rod McKuen poem.

It might have worked if someone had put out a pair of running trunks with tummy and thigh control, but there was no way I was going to show my legs from the knees up. I popped for a sixty-five-dollar pink velour warm-up suit.

The shoes were a little trickier. There were 147 styles, each of them priced from forty to eighty dollars. I chose a pair that gave me no arch support whatsoever but had pink shoelaces (can you believe my luck?) exactly the same shade as my pink velour warm-up suit. My handbag matched close enough.

The real zinger was the patch of lonely road. The street in front of my house was definitely out, as all the walkers were running from the dogs and the cars.

My husband told me to start a "training diary" of my distances and times and he would take me to the bike path by the canal.

The stitch in my side was sharp and persistent. I remembered that Mr. Fixit said, "No one ever died from a side stitch" and breathed deeply. I tossed in, "Thank you, stitch!"

"What did you say?" asked my husband.

I told him I had a stitch in my side, but if I considered it a friend it would go away.

He said it was probably my sunglasses that I had looped over my pants gouging me and that once we got out of the car the pain would go away.

We parked the car and I looked at the bike path. I had seen lonelier patches of road leading from Disneyland after the Fourth of July fireworks.

"Who are all these people?" I asked.

"They're roller-skaters, bikers, skateboarders, kite flyers, and joggers." It was easy to spot the joggers. They were all together in an ozone of liniment, bending and stretching and speaking fluent jogging to one another: "split times," "euphoria," "building up lactic acid and hitting the wall."

There was something different about them that I couldn't put my finger on at first. Then it hit me. There was no one there who weighed over nine pounds. I felt like stretch marks at a Miss America pageant.

A bicyclist whizzed by, nearly clipping a jogger. The jogger shook his fist and shouted at him "WEIRDO!" Somehow, the remark seemed incongruous coming from a man who was pasting adhesive bandages over his nipples to keep them from getting sore when they rubbed against his shirt.

A couple of hours later, I dragged into Edna's kitchen, where she was washing dishes. "What's the matter with you?" she asked.

"I'm not sure. I'm either experiencing a euphoric high or I'm catching flu. Can I have those leftover French fries?"

"I thought you had to watch your weight."

"I'm packing carbohydrates. I tell you, Edna, I'm exhausted trying to feel good about myself. All inner peace does is give me an appetite. Why am I telling you this? Everyone knows me like an open book."

"Not really," said Edna, rinsing plates and stacking them in the drainer to dry. "You are extremely conservative and guard your privacy. You take pains never to reveal anything about yourself so that other people have a hard time trying to help you."

"Who told you that?"

"No one had to tell me. I can tell by the way you always point your body toward the door and your knees and feet are rigid."

"Edna, my entire body is rigid because I am basted in Vaseline and I am suffering from Morton's Toe."

"What's Morton's Toe?"

"Jogging terminology. It means my second toe is longer than my big one and has turned purple and can fall off at any minute."

"Didn't anyone ever tell you you have bad body English?"

"BAD BODY ENGLISH? You're just trying to cheer me up."

"I'm serious. You show me a woman who sits like you do and I'll show you a woman who is sexually inhibited, defensive, withdrawn, and has a mind closed to new ideas."

"You can tell all that just by looking at me?"

"Sure. Why, I can tell you that Ralph there," she said, nodding toward her dog, "is unfulfilled, restless, and manifests his anxieties and frustrations in his actions."

I shook my head in disbelief. "That's really amazing. How did you figure all that out?"

"Ralph just wet on your shoe."

When I went home, I limped into the

bedroom and picked up my jogger's diary. On page one I put the date, wrote under it, "Erma hit the wall and went right up it," and slammed it shut!

Next to it on the bedside table was Jim Fixit's book. I studied the cover, then stood in front of the mirror and posed my legs like his. My forty-dollar shoes were spattered with mud and Ralph. The pink shoelaces hung limp. I had oil on my beautiful pink velour pants. I hiked up the pantlegs to see if my skin was taut, the muscles firm and the knees bony. My legs looked like an unpaved road with purple rivers running everywhere.

Easy for Mr. Fixit. He hadn't carried his babies low.

10

How to Tell Your Best Friend She Has Bad Body English

It was probably a coincidence that the carry-out boy looked at my license plates while loading the groceries and said, "I don't get it. What's TZE 403 stand for?"

"It's my license plates," I said.

"I know, but they don't make any sense."

"Are they supposed to?"

"Sure. You're the only driver I know who doesn't have something clever on her plates. Some kind of identification."

I looked up and down the line of parked cars. There were E-Z DUZ IT, I. M. CUTE, SAY

125

AAH, PAID 4, 2 CLOSE, CALL ME, I DRINK, and FLY ME.

"My Mom's got a neat set of plates," he said. "She's got 28-36-42. I know what you're thinking, but the good numbers were already taken." He slammed down the lid. "You don't even have a bumper sticker for anything. That's unusual."

On the way home, I checked out every car on the road. He was right. Just by looking at a car you knew who was for school levies, who they voted for, their religion, their alma mater, their club affiliation, their causes, and their issues. (I could hardly wait to pass the bumper and see who belonged to the sticker that read WOMEN NEED ATHLETIC SUPPORTERS TOO.)

Maybe Edna was right. Maybe I was overly zealous about my privacy. When I thought about it, I didn't have a CB in my car to carry on a conversation with other drivers. I had never named a house or a cabin something clever like "Dew Drop Inn" and had never worn my name in gold on a chain around my neck.

I didn't personalize my blouses, towels, or stationery with my initials or send out warm, intimate newsletters about our family at Christmas.

I wore a mood ring for two weeks once, but discarded it when I looked at my American Express bill one January and went into ring failure.

I was so opposed to nametags that once when a woman slapped a gummed label over my left bosom that said "Hello! My name is Erma!" I leaned over and said, "Now, what shall we name the other one?"

I didn't even have a telephone that answered with a clever recording that said, "Hi there. I'm really glad you called. At the sound of the beep, tell me where you're coming from and I'll call you back and tell you where it's at."

At the sound of the beep, I would go into cardiac arrest in an effort to say my name and read my own phone number off my own phone. (I once called my mother and found myself spelling my last name.) Another time I had a note to return a call and dialed the number. There was a slick voice that said huskily, "Hi, Honey. I told you you'd call. I'm out getting your favorite white wine. The key is in the usual place. At the sound of the tone, tell me what time you'll be here."

No one was a person of mystery any more.

The T-shirt craze had clearly gotten out of hand. In one day alone I encountered three propositions, four declarations, two obscene suggestions, and a word so bad I stopped the car and threw a blanket over the girl's chest.

Mother was with me one day when I stopped for a traffic light and a healthy blonde with jeans so tight her hipbones looked like towel hooks crossed in front of the car. Tucked inside was a T-shirt that read in large, bold letters SPACE FOR RENT.

We didn't say anything for a full minute. Then Mother observed, "You can say what you want, but she certainly is well read."

Well read, indeed. I could be clever if I

wanted to. My car license was up for renewal. Maybe I'd go for something kinky on my plates.

"How many letters do we have to work with?" asked my husband.

"Six," I said.

"Great," said my son. "How about BEWARE?"

"Or GAS HOG?"

"Aw, c'mon," I said, "I want a plate that won't have people passing me at seventy-five miles an hour just to see what kind of a nut is behind the wheel. I was thinking more of a plate that would give me character . . . a self-description that would be unique and apply only to me."

"How many letters in DRUDGE?" asked my son.

We must have sat there another two hours trying to get a six-letter combination. Finally I said, "I've got it. How about VIT B-12? What do you think?"

"I think you have just solved the problem of the kids ever borrowing your car again."

Having personalized license plates was a step forward in revealing my mystique, but I wasn't sure I wanted people sitting around reading my entire body. According to the book Edna loaned me (*Body English Spoken Here*) it wasn't that hard to do.

Women who crossed their legs in cold weather were announcing they wanted attention. In hot weather, they were bragging.

Doctors who tapped pencils were reassuring themselves they hadn't lost them during an examination.

Men who removed their wedding rings while attending a convention in another city were saying they didn't care whether they lived or died.

Women who covered the telephone receiver when they *listened* were hearing something they shouldn't.

Teeth closing in on a dentist's hand is definitely interpreted as a hostile act.

But it worked both ways. If I could learn Body English I'd be able to read what other people were thinking even if they did not utter a single word. There was an entire section on the subtle signs men and women who are on the make exchange that was absolutely fascinating.

This was a subject I couldn't even draw on from memory. It had been too long. I wouldn't know a pitch if I struck at it.

Body English Spoken Here made me an authority. I felt I could interpret any subtlety the opposite sex threw at me. I didn't have a chance to test it until one afternoon when Mayva and I stopped shopping to grab a bite of lunch.

At a table a short distance from us were two men who glanced our way.

"Don't look at them," I said without moving my lips. "I can tell you that men mentally raise the hemline of a woman's skirt six inches if she wears lipstick."

Mayva rummaged in her handbag. "Do I have any left on?"

"If you look them in the eye and their pupils dilate, you're in over your head."

"What other goodies do you know?"

"I know that when you are flirting your eyes become less baggy, your jowls firm up, your shoulders become straighter, and you suck in your stomach without thinking about it. And if you put on your glasses, you'll look more intelligent than you really are."

Mayva gave a sharp cry. "What am I saying? Quick? One of them is coming over toward us."

"Did you cross your legs?" I whispered loudly. "That's a come-on. Or unbutton your jacket? Or moisten your lips? Tell me you didn't moisten your lips."

"I don't think so," said Mayva.

"Then just keep your head down and we'll try to undo any message our bodies sent."

A shadow crossed the table and kept going.

Mayva looked at me with disgust. "I just read the body of the man that passed us. It said 'Don't get too choked up. I'm going to the men's room.'"

Mayva could really get on your nerves and despite what she thought I still believed knowing Body English was a real plus. Especially the part devoted to the Body English of teachers. Boy, did I need that. With two children still left in high school I had to admit I was lost without an interpreter.

I didn't know what had happened to education, but within the past several years it was getting tougher and tougher to speak the language.

It was simple back in the days when teachers spoke in polite language. I didn't need an interpreter to know that when Miss Meeks said, "Bruce's personal habits have shown marked improvement" she really was saying, "He no longer wets himself every day now that he has discovered the bathroom walls."

Or "I personally hope that your son develops more self-confidence" meant he copied on every test. I knew when she duly reported, "His paper on irrigation among the Barbizon tribe was far above that expected from a fourth-grader" it translated to "How long did it take you to write it?"

But in recent years I couldn't make head or tail of what they were saying. In fact, last year's conference had been a nightmare.

When I was seated at the desk, Mrs. Vucci polished her glasses and said, "Well, let's see here what we have in the way of comments from Bruce's other teachers. According to this report, Coach Weems says he has potential but is incapable of any viable feedback. That tells us, of course, that we have a child who does not relate to social interreaction."

I nodded numbly.

"Mrs. Wormstad says he is not motivated by curriculum innovation and they don't want him to stagnate in a lockup system and they're trying to stimulate his awareness. Mrs. Rensler writes he is having behavior modification problems and they're putting him in a modular-flexible schedule. Let's hope it works.

"I personally feel we have to consider the conundrum. But seriously," she said, "it's hard to say where the burden for apathy lies, but before his achievement levels polarize, we'll counsel Bruce so he can realize his potential and aim for some tangible goals."

I had not understood one single word she had said.

"Do you have any questions?" she asked, noting my silence.

I shook my head. She wouldn't have understood the questions and I wouldn't have understood the answers. What a pair.

With Body English I might at least stand a chance. Another teacher conference was coming up in a couple of weeks and I wanted to be ready for it.

My appointment was for seven-thirty and I was early. As I poked my head around the corner of the room, Mrs. Lutz said without looking up from her desk, "I know. We all dread these sessions, don't we?"

"How can you tell that?" I smiled.

"Your reticence to appear fully in the doorway instead of inching your way into the room."

I sat down on the edge of the chair. She looked over her half-glasses and said, "There is no need to be uptight. Just sit back and relax."

"I am relaxed," I said quickly.

"No one is relaxed sitting on the edge of the chair. And stop worrying, it's not that bad."

"I don't think it's bad."

"Of course you do," she corrected. "I can tell by the way your feet are coiled around the chair legs."

This wasn't working at all. She wasn't supposed to be reading my body. I was supposed to be reading *hers.*

But I couldn't help it. The more she talked, the harder time I had to keep my body from talking. When she brought out his essay on "The Anatomy of a Belch" I sank into a fetal position and lowered my head.

When she told me he not only parked his car illegally in front of the school but told the security people he thought they had valet parking, I made a necklace out of her paper clips and chewed at my cuticles until they bled.

By the time she told me his career tests showed his future lay in shepherding, I had used every bit of Body English in the book.

It was useless to play games. She asked me if my son and I related to one another. I said nervously only through a young marriage. She said that wasn't what she meant. She was trying to establish what kind of a parent-child relationship we had.

That's when it all came out. I told her none of my children understood parents my age. They talked to me but they never listened to what I had to say. They were always too busy. I stopped telling them anything because when I did I was always in for a lecture. They never took my side.

They blamed me for everything. Never let me assume responsibility for things I could do myself. All they did was criticize. (I leaned forward.) I think they even spy on me. "Miss Lutz," I said flatly, "they treat me like an adult."

She folded my son's manila folder and leaned back on her chair. "You're not the only parent who has problems with their children understanding them," she said. "There's a wonderful new manual out called *Bringing Up Parents the Okay Way.* I don't know whether or not you can get your children to read it, but at least you'll get a better understanding of why they do and say the things they do."

I started to stand up.

"Don't forget your feet," cautioned Miss Lutz, nodding toward my legs still coiled around the legs of the chair. "That could be interpreted as some very strong Body English."

I smiled smugly. "I read a little Body English myself," I said proudly. "As a matter of fact, while you've been observing me, I've been observing you. I have come to the conclusion you are an excellent teacher, secure, in command of a situation, and will be around here for a long time."

"Not really," she said, easing herself out of the chair. "I'm eight months pregnant and am going on maternity leave next week."

Some bodies are very deceptive.

11

Bringing Up Parents the Okay Way

The trouble with my kids is they had read too many books on Parent Psychology. They thought they knew all the answers, but the truth is they didn't know me at all.

They corrected my grammar in front of my friends, told me my clothes were too young for me, bugged me about my short hair, and never tried to relate to my problems.

God knows, I had problems. I wasn't popular and wasn't with the "in" group. The in group in my neighborhood were women my age who had reentered the job scene.

Every morning, I watched them from my window as they swung to their cars dressed in contemporary clothes and teetering in five-inch heels to their day in carpetland.

From my vantage point, I could only fantasize how they answered phones that weren't sticky, had lunch in a place with live plants, and talked to people who didn't respond with the same two words, "far out."

The high spot in my week was being invited to a luncheon style show where I pilfered five or six sample vials of perfume that lasted five or six minutes before the alcohol burned off.

The friends I liked my children weren't crazy about. They didn't like Yvonne, who was divorced and dated their former orthodontist, because they thought she was a bad influence on me.

They didn't like Gloria, who always came over at dinnertime and hung around while we ate, because she never seemed to have a home of her own.

And they didn't like Judy, who never cleaned her house and schlepped around in grubby clothes and greasy hair. (They said they had NEVER seen her cleaned up and she set a bad example for me.)

Sometimes I didn't know what the kids expected from me. When I needed them, they were never home.

When they were home they drove me crazy trying out their latest in parent-psychology techniques. I could always tell when they had a new theory they were trying out. I had their undivided attention.

They tried every new theory to come down the pike—active listening, effectiveness training, and transactional analysis.

I wasn't surprised to find the manual Mrs. Lutz mentioned, *Bringing Up Parents the Okay Way*, in a stack of magazines in the bathroom.

On the cover was a picture of a teenager with an insincere smile. He had put down his paper to give his attention to his mother, who was showing him something she had just read in a book.

I leafed quickly through a chapter called "How to Say No to Your Parents." I knew how. I just didn't know why. Then my eyes caught a heading called "The Middle-Parent Syndrome. What is your position in the Family?"

That was it. I was a middle parent. No wonder I was weird. I was neither the oldest nor the youngest. I was wedged in the twilight zone where no one ever does anything for the first time, says anything original, wears anything new, or is cute.

My position in the family car bore this out. When I was first married I snuggled up against my husband so close he looked like he was driving alone. When the first baby came, I moved all the way over to the door so the baby could sit between us. With the second child, I hung over the back seat and arrived everywhere fanny first so I could make sure they hadn't fallen on the floor.

With the third child, I lost my front seat and became a part of the back seat so that each child could have his own window.

When car pools became a part of my life, I was returned to the front seat, but as a steady driver. No one ever talked to me or for that matter acknowledged I was there.

When the kids began to drive, I was once more shuffled to the passenger side of the car.

Lately, I had been delegated once again to the back seat when I got a seat at all. I was on to something and I knew it as I feverishly thumbed my way to a chapter on "Growing Up." It said when we can stand alone without leaning on our children, we have indeed reached the age of independence.

It was confusing. I didn't know what I wanted. There were times when I wanted to be alone. Like when my friends dropped in. I remember one day Yvonne came by to tell me about Elaine's hysterectomy and before she could go into detail, my youngest parked himself between our coffee cups and observed, "Dogs get fat after their operation. I hope poor Elaine can hold her own."

There were other times when I wanted to be needed and leaned on.

I slammed the book shut. This particular day was definitely not one of those days. There were thirty-five unwashed glasses on the countertop by the sink. I didn't own thirty-five glasses.

The front door had not been shut all the way in two years. There were six cars in the driveway. One of them ran.

The baking soda I had put in the refrigerator to keep odors down was half eaten.

There were black heelmarks on the oven door.

The dog looked fat.

I wanted to say good-bye to pure, organic, honey-herbal scented shampoo that cost a dollar fifty an ounce and was at this moment on its side with the cap off running down the drain.

Good-bye to Linda Ronstadt and Billy Joel. Good-bye to porch lights that had to be replaced every six weeks. Good-bye to mildewed towels and empty ice-cube trays and labels that read HAND WASH ONLY. Good-bye to lunch meat that dried out and curled up because no one rewrapped it.

All my friends had shed the dependency of their children and were on cruises. I know because there wasn't a day one of them didn't write me.

I was still sorting socks, skimming crumbs off the top of the water jug in the refrigerator, and every Mother's Day feigning ecstasy over a cheese shredder.

One day as my older son was looking for his glasses so he could find my purse and the other one was rearranging the dials on my car radio to a rock station, I knew what I had to do.

I took him aside and said, "You know, as a child who didn't plan for parents, you've done a pretty good job. I know I've goofed up a lot . . ."

"If it's about the cashmere sweater that shrunk, forget it," he said.

"No, it's just that we can't seem to communicate any more. We always end up shouting."

"Mom," he said. "These are the best years of your life."

I started to cry. "Kids are always saying that. The point of this conversation is why can't you accept me and not my behavior? Why do I have to be perfect? I never seem to be doing what every other mother is doing at the same time she is doing it. The time has come for me to break away and be the person I was meant to be. I think you should move out and get your own apartment."

I left him mumbling "Where have I failed?"

The next night when Gloria padded in at dinnertime and took her chair, I told her of my ultimatum.

"You're a credit to parents everywhere," she said. "I hope you're covered by Teenage Apartment Insurance."

"What's that?"

"It's a new policy for parents of young people who leave to get their own apartments. The premiums are expensive, but they cover loss of furniture up to five thousand dollars, damages to cars hauling away contents of house and restocking of the refrigerator."

"You're kidding."

"And you've got a short memory," she said. "Remember how it was when your daughter went to school? You both rattled around in here without so much as a stick of furniture. The only thing she left was an echo."

My son must have known my fears, for a couple of weeks later when he said, "I've found an apartment," he added quickly, "Don't worry. It's furnished."

My relief lasted only until we looked at it. I've seen recovery rooms with more furniture.

"Do you need a skillet?"

"What for?" he chirped. "I'm only going to be eating one meal a day at home."

Somehow he instinctively knew the roast beef nights at home and came in like he was on radar. Occasionally on these nights he'd yell from another room, "Do you want this?"

"What is it?"

"The TV set."

"Of course we want it."

"You can have the green lamp back for it."

"This isn't a park-'n-swap."

Eventually he had it all . . . the afghans my mother had made, the dishes he borrowed for a party and never returned, the typewriter, the window fan, the big pot for spaghetti, the beach towels, the four-wheel drive, and the bicycle that "is just sitting there and someone will steal it and you'll never see it again."

What really hurt was we hadn't a dime's worth of Teenage Apartment Insurance to ease the loss.

Things eased up a little after he left, with only one child in high school, but it wasn't like having our own apartment.

Gloria was with me the afternoon he became disgusted with me for not having gas in my car which he was borrowing.

"Why do you take all of that?" asked Gloria.

"It's easier than arguing. Besides, he wouldn't yell at me if he didn't love me."

"Haven't you ever heard of assertiveness?"

"Of course I've heard of assertiveness. Are you saying I'm not?"

"I'm saying if you are, you could sure use a lot more of it. Your trouble is you don't know how to say no and do you know why?"

I shook my head no and hated me for doing it.

"It's because you're very insecure about yourself. You want to be loved and you don't want to take a chance on alienating people."

"You're wrong," I laughed.

"Okay, I want you to do something for me. I want you to go into the family room and announce 'This is my house. I am my own person. I am going to be more assertive.' "

I thought about it a second, then decided to call Gloria's bluff. I went to the living room where my husband and son were watching television.

"This is my house. I am my own person and I'm going to be more assertive."

My husband looked up. "I can't read lips. What are you mumbling about? Speak up!"

I cleared my throat and started again. "This is my house. I am my own person and I'm going to be more assertive."

"Son," said my husband irritably, "turn that sound down. Your mother is trying to say something. And hurry up. State is about to score."

"This is my house. I am my own person and I'm going to be more assertive . . . if it's okay with you."

12

Go Suck an Egg

I called it the E. F. Hutton Syndrome.

There wasn't a morning my husband did not sit at the table and read the entire newspaper out loud to me. When he read, everyone within a ninety-mile radius was supposed to stop what they were doing and listen.

He read me the editorials, the weather in Sharon, Pa., what Dear Abby said to the woman whose husband dressed in the closet, the sports scores, why South bid seven hearts, and what Lucy said to Charlie

Brown. (For no apparent reason, he made Lucy sound like Butterfly McQueen.)

The assumption was obvious. I could not read a newspaper by myself.

One day he started to read me a story of a dog who had found its way home after being lost for five years.

"Listen to this," he said. "A springer spaniel in Butte, Montana . . ."

"I read it already," I said.

". . . found its way home after five years when the family vacationed in . . ."

"The Everglades and was lost," I interrupted. It was like talking to a ballpoint pen.

"During his absence," he continued, "he served two years in the Army with distinction, saved a child from drowning and . . ."

"Made a drug bust in Nogales."

He looked up. "Did you know the dog?"

"I told you. I read it already."

"Well, why didn't you say so?"

My fantasy was one day to reach over with a pair of scissors and clip out the story he was reading, peek through the hole in the paper, and announce "I got my library card today."

Assertiveness had never been easy for me. In fact, I still wasn't convinced it wasn't congenital. You were either born with it ... or you weren't.

Whenever a salesperson tried to follow me into the fitting room, I always wanted to turn to her and say, "The last person who saw me in a pleated skirt went blind."

But I never did.

I always wanted to turn to my hairdresser and say, "If I wanted hair the consistency and style of a steel helmet, I would have been a Viking."

But I never did.

But most of all, I wanted to turn to Mildred Harkshorn one day and say, "Mildred, I've had it with you and your super kids who do everything first and better than anyone else. Do you know that I just read where there is a strong correlation between overachievers and the presence of venereal disease in the mother at birth?"

But I never did.

Mildred was a neighbor who had lived through the hedge from me for the past fifteen years with her husband, Leland, and their two children, Dwight David and Miracle. Miracle was a girl. Both could have been poster children for celibacy.

I liked Mildred. I really did. Our children had grown up together, but her kids had arrived late in her life and she somehow felt that since she took so long she couldn't settle for anything less than perfection.

They were born with capped teeth, snooze alarms, and a dry wish.

That set the pace for their entire lives.

They were toilet-trained at nine months.

Every time I misted my plants, mine lost control.

They were weaned off the bottle at one year.

Mine went through a dozen nipples a week—shredded by teeth marks.

Dwight David and Miracle received awards for music festival, cheerleading, football, scholarships, and science fair.

Mine got a free ticket for a hamburger

and a malt for bringing in fifty pounds of paper for the drive.

I couldn't get out of the school parking lot without Mildred tapping on the window and gushing, "I suppose your son told you about those awful SAT tests?"

My son had never spoken a complete sentence to me.

"I told Dwight David if he blew it he couldn't be captain of the baseball team. I don't care if he was elected unanimously by his teammates. His studies come first . . . by the way, did your son go out for baseball?"

My son wouldn't go out for the garbage unless we wrote him a check.

You have to be intimidated by a mother whose children never lied, never talked with food in their mouths, and wrote thank-you notes for a drink out of the garden hose when they played at your house.

If I were ever to become assertive, in my heart, I knew it had to begin with Mildred. She was at her mailbox one day when she yelled, "Hi there. How's your daughter doing at college?"

I smiled and walked over toward her. "Fine."

"What's that amusing name they call her again?"

"Suds."

"Here's another letter from Miracle," she said. "We're so close, you know. She writes me every day. Of course, I suppose your daughter does too."

"She probably dropped her Bible on her foot and can't get to the post office as often as she would like," I said.

"Maybe so," she smiled. "Some young people just simply don't feel a need for family. They view going away to school as an opportunity to break off all family ties and build an entirely new life for themselves."

I had fallen into her trap again and couldn't bring myself to talk back. What was wrong with me? Why couldn't I say what I felt?

As I walked back toward the house, I

saw Helen coming home from work. "Hello there," she yelled. "Hear from your college child today?"

I would not get caught again. "Oh, yes," I lied. "She writes every day."

"Is she still so dependent?" asked Helen, shaking her head. "Don't worry. She'll mature after a while and become adjusted. It just takes time for her to be her own person and not a mama's girl."

I couldn't win.

No matter what my children did, it was wrong. How come my kids were forgetful and everyone else's were "preoccupied"? Mine were fat, but other people's children were "healthy"? If mine were weirdos, theirs were "nonconformists." If mine were lazy, others were "deep thinkers." Mine flunked out, but other children were "victims of a poor teacher."

One night I was watching the Carson show when my husband told me I was sleepy and should go to bed or I'd be crabby in the morning. He turned out the light.

As I sat there wide-eyed in the semi-darkness watching the tube, Johnny introduced Dr. Eduardo Emitz, who had just authored a book called *Go Suck an Egg*.

There was no doubt in my mind that he was talking directly to me. He said being assertive isn't a luxury, it's our inalienable right. We don't have to feel guilty about it. We don't have to justify it. We don't even have to give a reason for it. Just do it.

He said there was no need to get emotional or hostile about stating your own mind. A simple way to get started was to make a list of things that bothered you and decide first how you were going to handle them. He promised you'd be your own person in no time.

I turned on the light and began to make a list of things that had to change:

I will no longer sit at the breakfast table and have the paper read out loud to me.

Smokers who blow smoke in my face will learn firsthand (within minutes actually) how injurious smoking can be to their health.

I will openly yawn in front of the next person who makes me a sexual confidante.

I will no longer hang on the phone waiting for Lynda to go back and applaud her son's BM's.

I will not collect from door to door for any disease I cannot pronounce.

I will not be upset by my mother-in-law when she calls me by my maiden name.

When I return something to the department store after Christmas, I will no longer wear black and tell them the recipient died.

When summoned to school I am going to assume my child is innocent until proven guilty.

Like Dr. Emitz said, you had to build up to assertiveness. It wasn't something you did in a day; you had to take one day at a time.

I started that night when we went to a restaurant to eat. As usual, I ordered my steak well done. When they brought it to the table, I thought I detected a heartbeat.

At first I toyed with the idea of pretending it was ham, but gently I put my fork down and said, "Please take this back and cook it a little longer."

"It won't be fit to eat," grumbled the waiter.

"In that case, I won't eat it," I said firmly.

Assertiveness felt good and the more I did it, the better I felt.

I demanded my butcher take the meat out from under the pink light and show me his prime rump in the daylight.

When Mayva pinned me down as to how I liked her new blow-'n-go hair style, I told her they didn't blow it far enough.

It was several weeks later when Mildred called to tell me how Dwight David found a flaw in his teacher's theory of relativity and publicly humiliated him in front of fifty students. I started to speak, but couldn't.

"You would think a twenty-year-old boy couldn't be smarter than a big-shot college professor with all those degrees, now wouldn't you? I swear I don't know where that boy gets it from."

"Mildred," I said, clearing my throat.

"Do you remember how excited you were when your son passed his eye examination?"

"MILDRED!" I shouted. "Do you know I've just read in a magazine where there is a strong correlation between overachievers and the presence of venereal disease in the mother at birth?"

I rarely saw Mildred after that. When I did she was always preoccupied and didn't notice me or remembered something she had to do and turned the other way. As a matter of fact, the more assertive I became, the less I saw of anyone, including my mother— whom I threatened with a tongue transplant from Rona Barrett if she didn't stop relating to the children all my past sins.

What the heck. At least I liked myself for my honesty. I had finally learned how to be a good friend to myself. When I thought about it, I was my ONLY friend.

I took me everywhere. To the movies. The zoo. Long rides in the country. I dined with me over intimate dinners and turned my head with flowers and candy. I knew I was getting too involved with me, but I couldn't seem to stop myself. We got along wonderfully. I knew when to talk to me and when to shut up. I knew when I was in a bad mood and when I wanted to be alone with just me.

I praised me when I did a good job and spoiled me outrageously. There wasn't anything I could deny myself because I was such a wonderful person. If anyone had a snout-full of self-esteem, it was me. People were beginning to talk and spread rumors about my extramarital affair with myself, but I didn't care. What I felt for me was genuine. (I think I even told me I wanted to have my baby.)

I had been my best friend for about four months when I began to notice little things about me that I had never noticed before. When I laughed, I snorted like a motor that had just turned over in a 1936 Chevy. At night in bed, I drove myself crazy flipping over the pillow looking for a "cool" side. When I argued, I smiled. Do you know how disgusting it is to argue with someone who smiles?

Not only that, some of my old habits of weakness were reappearing. Just a few days before I had let someone get in front of me in the express lane with a dozen items and said nothing. I hadn't really taken charge of my own life, I had only enjoyed a temporary attack of independence. I told me if I really loved me I could do anything I wanted. Every evening before going to bed, I did as Doctor Emitz had suggested. I stood in front of the mirror and said "I love you," to which my husband would always yell, "You say that now, but will you respect you in the morning?"

One morning when I asked me for a cup of coffee and answered, "Go get it yourself!" Mayva appeared and said, "Are you talking to yourself again?"

"What do you mean again?"

"You've been doing it for months now. You don't go out any more or have anyone in. You have no friends and no one calls. You just go around here mumbling 'I'm okay. I'm not too sure about the rest of you,' and there's no one here."

"Mayva," I sighed, "in these past months I have found out so many things about myself. Through self-analysis and psychological groping, I have discovered that I am basically a boring person." She tried to interrupt. "I mean it. The other night I was telling me an amusing story that I have laughed at a hundred times and right in the middle of it, I interrupted me and said, 'What's on TV?'"

Mayva put her hand over mine. "Anyone gets bored with herself if she thinks about herself all the time. It's called the 'Me-too-me-first Syndrome.' Don't you understand? Looking out for yourself is yesterday's leftovers. It used to be in, but now it's out. No one does that any more. Today the key word is commitment. Look around you. Everyone is into causes. Sometimes when you're out, just listen to people. They have goals . . . purpose . . . principles . . . something they believe in and are fighting for. The word today is involvement."

"You're kidding," I said. "You'd have thought I would have told me if things were changing."

"You've been so isolated," said Mayva, "you probably didn't know it. You've got to get out of this house again and start living . . . see people, go places, do things. Look, if your best friend won't tell you, I will. You're self-centered and shallow."

I looked in the mirror at my best friend for the past few months and waited for her to say something.

The truth hit me. I didn't love me that much!

13

A House Divided Against Itself Cannot Stand One Another

I missed me. When I had been my own best friend, I didn't have to dress up, go out, or sit around all night listening to someone else talk.

All I had to do was get up every day and take my emotional temperature. Did I love me more today than I did yesterday? Was I really in command of my own life? Could I con myself out of doing the hand laundry for another month?

I had heard about the Me-too-me-first phase. It happened to people who read too many how-to books and became terminally strange. Was it possible I had become too obsessed with myself?

If it was, maybe—by mingling in the world of what's happening—I could find a cause that appealed to me. What better way than to give a party? I'd simply invite a couple dozen friends and during the course of the evening, some cause or project would strike my interest and I could direct my energies away from myself.

As I made out the guest list, I reminisced about the days when you simply called up your friends, put a ton of food on the table, set out the booze, and let it happen. All that had changed.

If we invited John, we had to invite three other smokers who could stand with him defiant and unified against the rest of the room.

Stella drank only vodka, twelve guests were "into white wine," and the rest of them sanctimoniously hoisted French water with a twist of lime.

Eight were vegetarians, three would eat

nothing from the sea because it was tainted, and fifteen were on diets.

Lois drank eight glasses of water with her diet and had to have a straight shot at all times between her and the bathroom. Mary Ellen still had to weigh her portions on a postal scale. Elaine ran to test her urine every time she ate a carbohydrate, and Jerry brought her own concoction consisting of seaweed, olive oil, goat's milk, and cantaloupe which she stored in a Tupperware container in the refrigerator.

I couldn't seat a runner next to a lump, a nuclear proponent next to an environmentalist, a gun-control advocate next to a hunter, or a childless-by-choice next to a breast-feeder.

There should have been an easier way to get a handle on what was happening in the world and find a niche for myself.

When I saw Marj come in wearing a fur coat, I tried to propel her away from Liz, but not before Liz said in a loud voice, "My dream is to see an animal walk into a party some night dressed in a cape made out of Marj!"

I guided her into a conversation with George, who was arguing with Stan about the busing issue. I introduced Stan to Lois, who was in a shouting match with Doug about cohabital living. I thrust Lois into a group who were pro-abortion only to discover she was a Catholic, and then propelled her into a conversation with Stella. Stella, a feminist, was shouting at Sonya, who said she was happy staying home and why couldn't Stella accept that?

Liz appeared at my elbow and—nodding toward George—said, "What kind of a jerk would be against neutering animals?"

At the same time, Sonya complained she had a respiratory disorder and couldn't talk to a smoker, so I introduced her to Mary Ellen.

Doug said there wasn't one person at the party who read *The New York Times* and one woman thought a vasectomy was an operation for varicose veins. Was there no one who had an opinion on the Marvin decision!

When they were seated for dinner, my eyes glanced nervously around the table. Let's see, I had the natural-childbirth advocate next to the minister, the legalize marijuana next to open enrollment, jogger next to environmentalist, antiviolence next to the woman who didn't own a television set, the chauvinist next to the anti-feminist, and the anti-pay-toilet demonstrator next to . . . who else? Lois, who was on her seventh glass of water but couldn't tear herself away from her dinner companion's views.

The only thing I had forgotten was to put my husband, the left-hander, at the end of the table. Luckily, left-handers were pacifists.

Their conversation sounded like the Tower of Babel. Every once in a while words and phrases would surface loudly: "a new concept," "the bottom line is productivity," "at this point in time," "a positive interaction," "sexual freedom."

Mayva was right. I needed the stimulation of a cause that would put me on the other end of one of those conversations.

Later, as I was talking with Emily about volunteering a few hours a week at the Save the Whale Sperm Bank, Stella steered me to the sofa and said, "Let's talk."

She eased herself back into the cushions. "When are you going to take yourself away from all this?"

"I'm the hostess," I said simply.

"I don't mean the party. I mean all this domesticity."

I liked Stella. I also knew she never got too choked up over a "nice windy day that was perfect for drying blankets."

In fact, her wedding linens dissolved in the washer and her marriage dissolved in the courts the same week. She took that as an omen.

Like Helen, my neighbor, Stella had made the transition from the utility room to the board room as easily as napping during a piano recital.

"You're such a success," I smiled. "I'm so proud of you."

"And you could be a success too," she said. "It's a game. Men have been playing it for years. Have you read *Looking Out for You-Know-Who* by Robby Winner?"

"Stella," I said, "I just went through that number. It didn't work."

"How do you know it isn't for you? You couldn't have been serious about breaking out of the mold. Look at you!"

"Now, what's the matter with me?" I asked.

"My God, no one wears a slip any more."

"That's not true. I know a lot of women who wear slips."

"Under a see-through sweater? Get serious. Look, babe, why don't you come down next week to my office and we'll have lunch. We can talk some more. Besides, I want you to see where I work."

I had no intention of following up on Stella's suggestion until one afternoon at the Save the Whale Sperm Bank when I had hung up on my 187th obscene phone call, I called and told her I'd be by around one.

Stella was on the twenty-seventh floor of one of those office buildings that looks like it's awaiting a countdown. Her secretary led me into her office.

I had lived in smaller apartments. A huge desk held a phone with five buttons. There was a wall of bookcases and two African spears that crossed a shield on the wall behind her desk.

"I didn't know you went to Africa," I said.

"I didn't, sweetie; it's part of the trappings." She slid her glasses (the size of goggles) back over her head, giving her a Marlo-Thomas-in-the-convertible look.

"How long have you been wearing glasses?"

"I don't. Look, will you stop acting like Penny meeting Sky King for the first time? It's what I've been telling you. It's all in Robby Winner's book. You have to look like success and play the game. The tan came from a sun lamp so my clients will think I have the security to vacation in Florida during the winter. I never sweat because I wear

174

lightweight clothes all year round and keep the thermostat at sixty-two. Coffee?" she asked.

I nodded. Her secretary brought in one cup and set it down in front of me.

"Aren't you having any?"

She shook her head. "An urgent bladder is a sign of weakness. I never indulge. You use all the tricks, honey. That chair you're sitting in . . . it's three times smaller than mine and has a soft cushion that makes you sit lower than me. Gives me an advantage. The books are all paneling. This desk set wasn't presented to me in appreciation by anyone. I just had a plaque engraved last week and it looks like I'm a recipient of something."

"Are you saying all of this is contrived, right down to your attaché case?"

"The insides smell like egg salad," she shrugged. "I cannot believe you are so naive," she chided. "We're competing in a man's world and it's serious business . . . well, maybe not all of it."

"You know something," I said, leaning closer.

"No, I was just thinking about an office party we had the other night that was rather interesting. Kay had to take Mark home."

"Who's Mark?"

"You saw him when you came in. He's the little red-haired secretary to Ms. Hamstein in Research and Development."

"You mean he had too much to drink?"

"Kay told me he was running around with a Cadillac hood ornament in his hand, shouting 'Anyone here lose a Krugerrand?' "

"Is he married?"

"Of course he's married. He probably should be at home with the kids anyway. He doesn't have to work. His wife has a good job, but it's an ego thing."

"I think office parties should be legally outlawed. What purpose do they serve?"

"Kay says it's a nice thing to do, but I don't know. Women turn into beasts when they've had a drink or two. Can you imagine those women executives plying all those struggling male clerks with drinks they're not used to? Why, even Cecil Frampton was discoing all over the place. Oh, he's got a nice figure all right. Hides it under those leisure suits. But by the end of the evening he was calling Ms. Hathcock . . . get this . . . GLORIA! And Debbie was cruising around. Marriage certainly hasn't settled her down."

"What's wrong with that?"

"I'll tell you what's wrong. She left with the new office boy and she is old enough to be his mother. There is really something pathetic about a woman who refuses to act her age. Oh sure, it may be a way out of the mail room, but he has to live with himself."

There was a silence as she shuffled through her handbag looking for her lipstick.

"I had a big week," I said. "I colorcoded my leftovers."

You had to give it to Stella. She certainly made the transition from plastic plates to power city. But she was the exception. Most of my friends didn't have such a flashy set-up. One worked in the school cafeteria, another passed out sausage samples in a supermarket, another sold real estate, and Kathy was a Girl Friday for an insulation contractor.

I rarely saw Kathy any more. She lived by a timetable. Even her headaches were scheduled. The sun never set on an empty Crock Pot. She left the house at seven, returned at four-thirty, and her domestic schedule never missed a beat.

Kathy had certainly changed. When I knew her, she was possibly the most unorganized homemaker to ever come down the pike. She was always running out of staples like meat, milk, and toilet paper. Her gas gauge was always on E and her children were never born when she thought they were going to be. She had possibly the only twelve-month pregnancies in the history of obstetrics. Her return to the labor market was a surprise to us all. It happened one afternoon when she returned from the orthodontist. She and her husband talked it over and they decided that no way could he support two overbites on his salary.

We occasionally talked on the phone (where she answered mechanically, "Brunwilder's Insulation, Kathy speaking"), but I hadn't been to visit her since she returned to work. I didn't know the place.

Just inside the door was a large mirror. Over it was a lettered sign that read STRAIGHT TEETH MEAN SACRIFICE.

The house was decorated in Early Memo. You couldn't see the refrigerator door for the instructions on it.

- NOW HEAR THIS. . . . When the floor becomes adhesive, MOP IT.
- There is no known navy-blue food. If there is navy-blue food in the refrigerator, it signifies death.
- Setting the table is not considered child abuse.
- Anyone eating an entire can of albacore white tuna packed in water for a snack must be prepared to work out financial arrangements.
- An open refrigerator door and the

furnace going at the same time are in-compatible.
• Look upon one glass carried from your bedroom to the kitchen as "one small step for man, one giant leap for mankind."
• Today is a new day. Throw away something off the countertop.
• The dog's business is EVERYONE's business. Even when you don't see it, clean it up.

In the utility room was another memo:

• You are standing in a utility room.
• Clothes are washed, dried, and ironed here.
• Hand washables left over ten years will be sold.
• Spaghetti inside the washer can be traced.
• Small brown dots on clothes that smell like a wet possum should be dealt with immediately.
• Match every sock with something. Color, texture, and size is not im-portant.
• Do not shake out gym clothes as

they trigger the smoke alarm. Process them immediately.

• Do not take the chill off the room by turning the iron to the COTTON setting.

• One pair of jeans is considered a "mini" load.

• Clothes do not have feet. They cannot skip, run, or walk. They must be carried to your respective bedrooms.

The bathroom memo read:

• Towels in the bathroom are yellow. REPEAT. Yellow. If they appear in any other color, drop them into the nearest clothes hamper.

• A word about gravity. A shampoo bottle when lying on its side with the cap off will eventually empty into the drain. Just because there's 35 pounds of hair in the drain, there is no need to shampoo it.

• Flushing is an equal-opportunity job. Simply press finger firmly on the lever and push. If water "runs" longer than 15 hours, jiggle lever gently.

• Hair dryers left on and shut up in a

drawer serve no purpose. Turn them off.

• The management requests you conserve towels. No more than one for hair, one for the right arm, one for the left, and one for the body. Somewhere, there is a war on.

• The mystery of disappearing soap has been solved. A discovery made in 1903 revealed soap, when submerged in water, will dissolve.

• FIFTY MINUTE SHOWERS CAUSE ACNE.

After visiting with Stella and Kathy the thought of going home was depressing. My surroundings didn't exactly have the stamp of success written all over them. My meat always overthawed and ran down the stove. There was a mountain of "hand washables" in the utility room with baby sweaters near the bottom. Someone had written in the dust on the coffee table, "For a good time call Leah 555-3049." I cannot remember when there was a pencil by the phone.

Why didn't I take pride in my work?

Homemaking, if you did it right, was just as creative, just as vital, and just as professional as what women were doing outside the home. Besides, it was one of the few jobs left where you could have an urgent bladder and not lose respect.

As for the extra money they made, I could run my home like a business if I tried. Why, I could save thousands of dollars just passing up convenience foods, clipping coupons, saving stamps, pumping my own gas, and grooming the dog.

Could there be a book on how to run a home more efficiently and save money? Does the Pope work Sundays?

The phone rang at the Save the Whale Sperm Bank. I listened for a minute or two, then said, "If you knew ANYTHING about whales, sir, you'd know that is physically impossible!" and hung up.

14

Living Cheap

The bookstore was bulging with books on how to save money. It seemed strange to me that they were on a table marked Current Fiction.

Leading the list was the current best seller, *How to Dress a Chicken* (From Separates to Basic Weekenders), followed by *How to Perform Home Surgery Using Sewing Basket Notions*, and my favorite, *How to Build a Summer Cabin Using Scraps Ripped Off from the Neighborhood Lumber Yard.*

I didn't want to get too specific. I just

wanted a general book on how to save money by doing things around the house myself. The clerk recommended one that had been selling briskly called *Living Cheap*.

The book cost $23.95, but she said if I followed the advice in the first chapter alone, I'd recoup my original investment in a week.

The first chapter told me if I saved coupons I could cut down on my food bills as much as twenty dollars a visit. They were wrong. The first week, I saved thirty dollars using coupons that I had clipped from every paper and magazine that came into the house.

By having coupons I got an extra carton of cat food . . . an extra bucket of swimming-pool chemicals . . . an extra carton of infant strained lamb . . . and a huge savings on calf's liver.

The only problem was we didn't have a cat, a swimming pool, or a baby, and we all hated liver.

Double-stamp hours made a lot of sense. If I went to the store between 7:30

and 8:45 on a Wednesday morning following a holiday and was among the first ten shoppers to buy the manager's special and come within two minutes of guessing when the cash register tape would run out on the express-lane register, I'd receive double stamps, which when the book was filled would give me ten cents off a jar of iced tea that made my kidneys hurt.

I licked and pasted until the family said my mouthwash just wasn't cutting my glue breath.

I tried creative things with my leftovers, disguising everything with a blanket of cheese and a sprinkling of parsley to kill the taste.

Some of the suggestions were just not practical, like "Don't shop when you're hungry," which eliminated all the hours when the store was open.

I soon tired of trying to disguise cheap cuts of meat to look like something wonderful. (The chicken necks lashed together like a Polynesian raft set adrift on a sea of blue-tinted rice just didn't do it for me.)

Moving quickly to Chapter 2, I discovered I could create an exclusive health spa in my own home for pennies. If there was anything I needed help on it was my body. I neglected it shamefully. The only equipment I had was a phone that rang every time I got into a hot tub.

At the shopping center I decided to blow a few bucks on one of those pulley exercisers that you attach to your doorknob.

Fifteen minutes a day, said the directions, was all it took to lose inches. It was midafternoon when I started to mix together all the concoctions to restore my youth.

First, to give my hair shine, I separated three eggs, beat the yolks with the juice and grated rind of a lemon, and massaged it into my hair. I topped it off with egg whites which had been beaten stiff.

Next, two bunches of mint leaves were blended with body lotion and applied to my face and entire body. Slipping a towel over me, I opened the refrigerator door and removed a bowl of ripe avocados to which olive oil had been added and plunged my fingers into them to make my nails hard. The last thing I did as I stretched out on my back on the floor was place a sliced cucumber over each eye to tighten the skin.

Attaching the pulley to the door, I slipped my wrists into the loops of the exerciser. Slowly at first, I stretched my arms down to my side and felt my mint-covered leg being pulled up over my waist.

I must have lifted and lowered my legs for five or ten minutes when I experienced pain—pain that can only be caused by a door slamming into my skull.

"Anyone home?" asked my husband. He always looked at me when he said that.

I tried to sit up, but a cucumber slid down into my towel.

"I was going to ask if you were all right," he said, "but I have just answered my own question."

"You don't understand," I said. "I have just saved fifty or sixty dollars in beauty treatments at some expensive spa. I am using the secrets of the stars."

"Don't look at me," he said. "I won't tell a soul what I have just seen. Is there dinner? Or are you it?"

I got to my feet, clumsily clutched my towel, and started toward the shower. "That's the thanks I get for trying to save you money. I've been working my fingers to the bone scrimping and saving and doing things around here myself just to cut down a little on expenses and that's the thanks I get."

"I know," he said. "And I loved the chicken-neck rafts. It's just that if you really wanted to help and save money, you could start with the car."

"What do you want me to do for it?"

"For starters, you could learn how to use the self-service islands. That would save a couple of pennies per gallon. And when gas is scarce, you could take time out of your day and have the car gassed up. That would really help."

He didn't know what he was asking. He was talking to a woman who, every time she tried to pull on the car lights, inadvertently released the hood. A woman who had driven for years with the rear-view mirror turned in at lip level. He was talking to a driver who started to pull out of a gas station one day when a man knocked loudly on the car trunk.

When I jammed on the brakes he said, "Ma'am, here's your gas cap. They forgot to put it on."

"Thank you," I said, dropping it into my handbag.

"Aren't you going to put it on your gas tank?"

"If I were," I asked cautiously, "where would I put it?"

I couldn't remember the last time I got gas. He had been getting it to and from work, so I mentally blocked out fifteen minutes on my schedule to pop in and pop out.

Thinking I was in a right-turn lane of cars, I eased around the thirty or forty cars ahead of me and pulled in just in front of a Volkswagen convertible. The man in the car jumped out and tapped on my window.

"Whatya think we're in line for? Demolition Derby?" I had seen that look on a face only once before and vowed I'd never forget it. It was a movie with Rod Steiger, who was playing the part of Pontius Pilate just before he sentenced Jesus of Nazareth.

"Don't worry," I smiled. "I'm not in the full-service line. I'm pumping my own gas."

I think it was then that he threatened to braid my lips. I took my place at the end of the line and played the radiator game with the rest of 'em. (Each one chipped in a quarter and the one whose radiator boiled over first got the pot.)

Several hours later when I pulled to the pump, a guy with a clipboard said, "What time is your appointment or are you a standing?"

"A standing what?" I asked.

"A standing appointment for your gas."

"You're kidding."

"No. We take a certain number of appointments per day. There's a shortage of gas, you know."

"I'll tell you what. If you'll fill my tank

I'll give you a four-piece place setting, consisting of a dinner plate, bread-and-butter plate, and a cup and saucer of the popular Toughware in the wheat pattern."

He relaxed his clipboard and picked his teeth with a matchbook cover.

"Wait a minute. If you put in ten gallons, I'll give you a Styrofoam cooler and a set of glasses with baseball heroes of the forties complete with signatures."

When he started to walk away shaking his head I yelled, "How about a rainbonnet in a handy travel case and balloons for your kids?"

With a lot of luck, I had just enough gas to make it home. I had blown three hours for nothing. I couldn't believe it. There weren't any impulses left in the world any more. Every Thursday, the beauty shop; every six months, the dentist; every year, the gynecologist; every April, H & R Block; every three months, my son's guidance counselor; every five weeks, the Avon lady; every Thursday, garbage day; every three hours, the grocery.

Now I was saddled with a 3:30 P.M. odd-numbered day every other week except when the month had five weeks in it, standing at the gas station for a fill-up, tune-up, lube job, and tire check.

No wonder my husband wanted me to take on the car. It was a full-time job.

A lot of my friends talked about the energy crunch and how it was affecting their lives. Most of all, the crisis was reflected in how far they could go for their vacations.

According to *Living Cheap*, there was an answer to the problem. You simply planned a wonderful "at home" vacation.

Imagine, no turning off 138 necessities of life, leaving instructions for your neighbors, jamming the family into a car, and setting off for Mosquito Larvae Lake or Kneespread, Texas, to God knows what awaits you.

No husband hostile because he could only make ten miles a day. No children hostile because their knees touched. No mother hostile because all she had to look forward to was a handbag full of quarters in a flying-lint laundromat.

My husband was suspicious about an "at home" vacation, but my son was downright surly. I told him: "How would you like to vacation in a place with great weather, two ovens, good food, a bedroom for everyone, TV privileges, and indoor plumbing? Close to swimming facilities, shopping areas, and all your friends?"

"It sounds like home to me," he grumbled.

"Let us think of it as Disneyland," I smiled. "The kitchen is Adventureland, the utility room is Frontierland, the garage is Tomorrowland, the bathroom, Main Street, U.S.A., and the bedroom, Fantasyland."

"We can take a lot of minitours and see our own state," I added, "and for the first time relax and get to know one another when we aren't racing around in a tense crisis situation. And look at all the money we'll save."

The first day of the vacation, I had a few chores for my husband, just to "pull the house together," that he had been putting off.

This included fertilizing, rolling, seeding, and mowing the lawn, adjusting the TV antenna on the roof, painting the exterior of the house, installing a humidifier in the crawl space in the hall closet, wallpapering two bedrooms, fixing a leak behind the washer, and—if there was time—stripping the kitchen cabinets and staining them a lighter color so the kitchen wouldn't seem so dark.

On the morning of the second day, I received a phone call from Mona and Dick Spooner from Billings, Montana, and their two little boys, Ricky and Richie.

They were passing through town when Mona remembered her old friend whom she had not seen since nursery school. When I asked her who the old friend was she said it was me. Naturally, I invited them to stay a few days.

They unloaded five years of laundry, fifteen suitcases, and a cooler that leaked water on my wax buildup.

During the next three days we became authorities on the Spooners.

The boys were just learning English and had not gotten to the three most beautiful words in the English language, "Close The Door!"

We discovered Richie could bounce a ball steadily against the house for 146 hours without stopping.

Dick was a finalist in the gargling Olympics.

Mona's only mental stimulation was sitting in front of the TV set in her baby-doll pajamas trying to answer the questions put to guests on *The Newlywed Game* and turning to Dick saying, "Am I right, baby?"

Ricky would not drink water out of a glass until it had been wrapped in transparent wrap like the motels.

Richie liked to throw rocks in the toilet because it bubbled when he did that.

Mona was allergic to domesticity and let me do the laundry because she wasn't "into electricity."

Sticky . . . I mean Ricky swiped a

pillowcase full of our knickknacks (seashells, ashtrays, and coasters) and stuffed them under the spare tire of their station wagon so we didn't know how to reclaim them without a scene.

The Spooners stayed for four days, which just about took us to the end of our vacation. The visit—counting short trips, entertainment, extra food and drink, and an eighty-dollar plumbing bill to turn off the bubble machine, set us back $450.

Somehow *Living Cheap* lost its credibility for me after the Spooner Experience. I didn't feel like buying clothes secondhand, shopping garage sales, or haunting park-'n-swaps.

I was bored with being clever. Who cared if I saved all the little containers of hot sauce from Mexican carryout or painted my varicose veins in Crayolas to make everyone think I was wearing textured stockings? No one.

Mother was visiting one afternoon when she saw the book on the back of the commode in the bathroom.

"Whose *Living Cheap*?" she asked as she came down the hallway and entered the kitchen.

"No one's any more," I said. "I'm out of my Brand X period and am between self-improvements at the moment."

"If you ask me, there's never been anything wrong with you that a little organization couldn't cure. You're always running around at the last minute like a chicken with her head cut off . . . going in nine directions. You can't seem to get it together."

"I do all right."

"Do you want to go through your entire life being 'all right'? Have you ever been on time for anything? Never!" she said, answering herself.

"If you heard the 'Star-Spangled Banner' you wouldn't recognize it. You've never seen a first inning, a first race, the first act, or the opening of anything in your life.

"Look at this house . . . coffee cups in every room . . . stacks of magazines

. . . shoes under everything . . . dog dishes in the living room . . ."

"It's a candy dish."

"The dog's eating something out of it. Did you get that little brochure about a course at the high school at nights called 'Tidying Up Your Life' or something like that? You ought to look into it. Lord knows you could use some help. When was the last time you tossed out the notes on your refrigerator door?"

"Mother! I'll thank you not to come in here and criticize the way I keep my house. If you must know, every time I come in I check the refrigerator for messages. I read them and throw them away."

She moved in closer to the refrigerator and removed a card that was yellow and faded. "Did you overlook this reminder to take your Edsel in for service? It says here they'll give you a full tank of gas and a set of dishes if you act before June 30, 1959."

15

Tidying Up Your Life

I was late for the Tidying Up Your Life class.

But it wasn't my fault. The roast was frozen when I put it in the oven at five, there wasn't a clock in the house with a time that matched, and two traffic lights were against me.

Luckily, the class was being held at the high school near me. I eased into a seat by the door and looked around. There were a dozen or so adults who had gathered to put some system back into their lives.

The woman across the aisle smiled and

whispered "I'm Ruth." Her socks didn't match.

A man behind me asked if I had a pencil he could borrow. Another man asked to be excused as he had left his car lights on.

It was obvious I did not belong here. They were all a bunch of losers who couldn't function with any semblance of order or priorities in their lives.

I shuffled through my handbag and finally resigned myself to reading without my glasses what the teacher, Ms. Sontagg, had written on the blackboard. It was a quiz on how organized we really were. One set of questions was for the men, the other for the women. We were to score one to twelve points for each answer.

1. Are candles in your house a touch of romanticism or the major source of light because you forgot to pay your utility bill?

2. Are you still living out of moving cartons when you have been in your home [check one] ( ) five years ( ) ten years ( ) fifteen years or more?

3. Can you put your hands on the Christmas cards you bought for half price in January?

4. Is your mail stored in one spot or do you use it as a dustpan when you sweep the kitchen floor?

5. Do you put groceries away after each visit to the store or use them directly from the car?

6. Do you often misplace things you use regularly—like door keys, handbags, glasses, or children?

7. Do you forget important occasions like birthdays, dental appointments, rabies shots for the dog, or Christmas?

8. Can you open your closet door without hurting yourself?

9. Would you feel comfortable letting guests wander through your house unattended?

10. Do you accomplish what you want to in a given day or are you always asking "What day is this?"

I leaned over to borrow Ruth's glasses

(they were held together with a paper clip) and answered the questions the best I could. My score was deplorable. But that didn't prove anything.

I got by. After all, I had been a writer from my own home for over fifteen years and never missed a deadline. That kind of discipline was bound to take its toll on my personal life. It certainly accounted for the sign on my front door, HOUSE OUT OF ORDER.

Ms. Sontagg said that during the next week we should try to pull together one facet of our daily routine and make some order out of it. In other words: Think Organization.

I walked out with Ruth, who offered to drive me to where my car was parked. (She had also arrived late and had parked her car in a towaway zone.) We discussed our frailties.

"The trouble with me," said Ruth, "is I'm a perfectionist. Do you have a coathanger?"

"What for?"

"I locked my keys in the car. I'm one of

those people who can't settle for mediocrity," she explained, taking off her necklace and making a loop in it to pull the button up. "Easy now . . . I got it!" she smiled. "Do you know I even used to iron diapers? The only reason I'm taking this class is so I can learn how to compromise. If I don't, I'm going to drive myself crazy. What's your problem?"

"It's my mother," I said. "She thinks I need organization. She plans her next headache."

Ruth nodded. "I know the type."

"Her spices are alphabetized. She cleans splatters from her stove every time she uses it. Every year she changes her closet over from winter to summer."

"You're kidding!"

"No. I have never seen my mother carry a suede handbag in the summer. She's what I call a box-saver."

"What's that mean?"

"It's the difference between youth and old age, I think. When you're young you believe that somewhere around the next bend is always a box when you need it. Old age never wants to take that chance."

"You know, I think you're right," nodded Ruth.

"She's got boxes inside boxes. I've received scarves in a stationery box, a blouse in a shoebox, and once on my birthday I got a small pendant in a box marked 'Rectal Thermometer.' Every Christmas, I get something from Mother in a Nieman-Marcus box. It's the same box. My Mother has never been in Nieman-Marcus in her entire life.

"Neat little boxes . . . stacked neatly in her neat little closet," I rambled, "boxes for transporting cakes, hamsters, laundry, and picnic supplies. Boxes for mailing. Boxes for storing. Boxes for starting fires. Boxes for sleeping dogs, snapshots, and memorabilia. Boxes for rainy-day projects. Boxes for boots by the door. Boxes to keep the baked beans from spilling over the car trunk. Boxes for a child's birthday present . . . boxes in boxes. . . ."

"Well," said Ruth, "it's been nice talking to you. See you next week in class."

"I guess so," I hesitated.

"The first rule of being organized," smiled Ruth, "is to keep an appointment book with you at all times." She took out a little green leather book titled CALENDAR and leafed through to the date. "Let's see," she said, "next Tuesday would be the sixteenth and the class starts at seven. I told you I'm a perfectionist," she said, slamming the book shut.

Under CALENDAR . . . embossed in gold . . . was the year 1976.

At the second session of Tidying Up Your Life, I looked for Ruth, but she never appeared. It was too bad, because we dealt with something that had long been a mystery to me: how to make the paperwork easier around the house.

I had a desk, but it was always cluttered and I mixed my business and personal papers together.

My checkbook hadn't been balanced in years.

Ms. Sontagg's suggestions were exciting. She said that for every check I wrote I should be recording it in a little booklet that fit right inside my checkbook. There was space on it for the date, the check number, who it was written to, and the amount.

Now, wouldn't you have thought that someone would have come up with that idea years ago? It certainly simplified knowing what your balance was at all times.

Ms. Sontagg gave us a home assignment. She said during the next week she wanted us to clean out one closet. "Be ruthless," she warned. "Throw out and keep nothing you are not using. We all have a tendency to accumulate things we don't need, but are reluctant to throw away. Do it!"

As she talked, I knew what I had to do. Clean out my husband's closet. It was a storehouse for all seasons.

Every time I opened the door it was like being in a time capsule. His first pair of long trousers. His knickers that he received his First Communion in. His double-breasted suit that he graduated in. His Nehru jacket. They were all there, along with his double-runnered ice skates, bowling ball, kite, composition books from college, old report cards, roadmaps (listing the original thirteen colonies), and fifteen years of back issues of teachers' magazines.

He had a thing about his possessions. Once I tried to pack for him for a vacation and he became quite testy and told me he could do it himself. His luggage weighed a ton. It should have. He was prepared for any occasion. If he won the Nobel peace prize, he had the clothes for it. If he was taken prisoner, he had the clothes for it. He could commandeer a torpedo boat through a squall, barter clothes for mules and guides into a remote jungle, and he had the wardrobe for it. He carried clothes for snorkeling, discoing, safaris, high teas, low ceilings, clothes for lounging, and clothes to leave behind as tips.

In tossing out his clothes I followed the three basic rules to a tee. (1) Have I used or worn it recently? (2) Will I ever use or wear it again? (3) Does it have any sentimental value to me?

Since it was his closet, the decisions were relatively simple.

It was with a feeling of exhilaration that I called a local organization that employed reformed gamblers and had an outlet store for used merchandise. They backed up the truck and I waved good-bye to clutter.

I knew the exact moment my husband discovered what I had done. You could have heard him in the next county. "What have you done with my clothes?"

"I have sent them to that big Trick or Treat in the sky."

He shook his head slowly. "Not my pants with the pockets in them? Not my lucky sweater that I was wearing when the war ended? Not my penny loafers?"

He needn't have carried on so. Within a week, the truck was back with all the items from his closet with a note saying "We're needy . . . not desperate."

I missed a couple of sessions of Tidying

Up Your Life, but when I went back for the last meeting I saw Ruth.

"Where have you been?" I asked.

"I told you I'm a perfectionist," she said. "I went home from the first class and started to dress all of my daughter's naked dolls. It took longer than I thought. Are you getting your life together?"

I assured her I was. My turkey roaster was stored on a shelf so high you got nosebleed from it. I had hooks on every door in the house, shelves in every bit of closet space, and was so efficient I was putting sanitized strips across the johns every time I cleaned them. I even ventured into my son's bedroom.

"How long has it been since you were in there?"

"Nineteen seventy-six. He had flu."

"How old is he?" asked Ruth.

"He's a senior in high school."

"Then he'll be going away to school next year?"

"I guess so. We haven't talked about it. I'm afraid I don't relate to my son very well.

211

He's the last one at home and we seem to come from different worlds. Somewhere I've failed him."

"Good grief! You put hooks on his doors and a basketball hoop over his clothes hamper. What does he want from you? Socks that match?"

"He doesn't want anything. That's the problem. It's probably my fault he doesn't spend more time at home. When he's there all I do is yell at him. I complain because I have to pick up after him all the time."

"What's wrong with that?"

"I yell at him for coming in late. I yell at him for wrecking the car. I yell at him for not getting a job. I yell at him for bad grades."

"So what's the problem? You want more choices?"

"You don't understand, Ruth."

"Oh, I understand all right," she said. "You're suffering from terminal guilt. How do you want to be remembered when you go? With a tombstone that stands upright and is chiseled with A MOTHER WHO CARED

Tidying Up Your Life

ENOUGH TO NAG or one that lies flat on the ground like a doormat with a WELCOME so everyone can step on it?

"You're on a guilt trip, my friend, and it's time you started living your own life. You should be like me. Two years ago I saw the light. I had just finished reading a book called *I'll Give Up Guilt When I Stop Making You Feel Rotten*. My son was cooking breakfast one morning when he broke the yolk in his egg. He yelled, 'Mom! Here's another egg for you to eat' and proceeded to break a fresh egg into the skillet for himself. At that moment I came to terms with myself. I announced, 'From this day forward, I am never going to eat another egg with the yolk broken.'"

"That's a beautiful story," I said.

"And it could be *your* story. Things are changing. We don't have to feel guilty any more about things that are supposed to be. Get the book and read it. Listen, it's been fun. I don't know about you, but I've gotten a lot out of this class. From here on in, my life is going to be orderly. I'm going to think before I talk; plan before I act; act before I procrastinate. I think I've got it all together now. So long, Edna."

"That's Erma," I said.

16

I'll Give Up Guilt When I Stop Making You Feel Rotten

I'd been giving a lot of thought to my tombstone lately and was torn between

IF YOU DON'T HAVE A HAIRCUT I CAN'T HEAR YOU

or

OVERDOSED ON IRON AND RUSTED TO DEATH 19—

Ruth had mentioned the word I never wanted to hear or for that matter deal with, *guilt*. She didn't know it but I was an authority on guilt. Had there been a Guilt Olympics, I could have won the Decathlon hands down. All ten events:

1. The ten-ring dash for the telephone call from Mother. Why did I instinctively know it was from her and let it ring while I got a cup of coffee and a calendar before I picked up the receiver?

2. The kitchen-table broad jump. Whenever anyone looked around and noticed salt/steak sauce/mustard/catsup/sugar bowl or anything missing, I jumped up like a gazelle and ran for it like I had springs in my underwear.

3. The thirty-minute nap. When I heard a key in the door, I'd jump up, throw cold water on my face, smooth my clothes, pull the bedspread taut, stagger into the kitchen, and throw an onion in the oven. When my husband mentioned the chenille marks on my face, I'd lie and say, "It's bad skin."

4. The finish-off-the-leftovers event.

Sometimes, I'd do a bypass right at the table where, instead of scraping the leftovers off into the disposer, I'd stuff them down Erma. Other times, I'd put them in a holding pattern in the refrigerator and try to inhale all of them by the next "grocery day."

5. The Sunday-night "paper due on Monday" dash. Faced with a child with a paper that had been assigned on the first day of school but had been put off, I felt obliged to borrow reference books on "The History of String" from a person who lived across town on a street that changed names three times after you left the expressway.

6. The draperies-can-be-cleaned-again-and-they'll-look-like-new hurdles. For six years I sacrificed new draperies for baton lessons, a root canal, ten-speed bicycle, low-calorie camp, classical guitar, and two snow tires.

7. The new-puppy throw-up. Despite repeated opposition to a new puppy, I gave in and ended up with a new lifestyle: contemporary dog hair with wall-to-wall urine and a barking doorbell.

8. The javelin throw through the heart. The first one home in the evening would look me straight in the eye and say, "Anyone home?" When I'd say, "I'm home," they'd say emphatically, "I mean ANYBODY!"

9. The non-Mother billfold. I'd want to die every time someone whipped out a billfold that unrolled like a giant tongue with 187 snapshots of their children. As I rummaged through a half stick of gum, a claim check for the parking lot, a piece of material I was matching, and a Kennedy half dollar, I'd explain lamely, "I sent my children's pictures out to be cleaned."

10. Fifteen-hundred-meter run. From wherever I was, I threw in my hand/ran up the aisle/stopped the game/stopped eating/quit talking/and hit for home so I could be there when I heard those wonderful words of praise from my children: "You'd better be home. I forgot my key."

I figured out long ago that guilt was like mothers. Everyone in the world had at least one. And it was passed down like a torch to the next generation. When you thought about it, a mother traditionally cried at weddings, but when there was a birth, there was always that crooked little smile on her face that said, "You're about to get yours."

I didn't have a friend who hadn't heard of her mother's thirty-six hours of hard labor, her stretch marks that would never tan, and how their appearance in this world at the same time as the Depression was "probably a coincidence, but we'll never be sure, will we?"

By the time I was twenty-five I had a list of things I was going to regret for the rest of my life that covered a wall.

"If you let that baby cry while you polish your nails, you're going to regret it for the rest of your life."

"If you don't get out of that bed and take an antibiotic and go to school to see Andy dressed as a grain of wheat in the Thanksgiving pageant, you are going to regret it for the rest of your life."

"If you don't curse gravy and become a born-again cottage-cheese disciple, you are going to regret it for the rest of your life."

"If you don't go with your husband on that fishing trip to Raw Waste Lake, where the cabin has a wood stove and the land temperature is 92 degrees and the lake temperature is 50 and has leeches, and pretend you are having a good time, you will regret it for the rest of your life."

If I had a dental appointment, I felt guilty. If I was sleepy and had to go to bed early, I felt guilty. If we ran out of toothpaste, I felt guilty. If someone asked me for the time and my watch had stopped, I felt guilty.

I apologized to the washer repairman who removed a pair of training pants out of the hose for forty-two dollars for not having the child toilet-trained.

I apologized to a baby sitter for not having better television reception and fresh lemon for her cola.

I even apologized for bothering a recording that told me to call back the next day when the office was open.

Of all the sins I committed in the name of sanity, possibly none was regarded with so much loathing and disgust as the mother who did not get up in the morning to get breakfast for her family.

It was unthinkable . . . un-American . . . and downright unconscionable.

I had always thought if training films were shown to brides contemplating marriage, the one that would have saved a lot of them from embracing matrimony would have been the one on the mother getting her family out of the house in the mornings.

It was a study in guilt.

I got blamed when the milk was warm and the bread was frozen and the kitchen floor was cold on their bare feet.

It was my fault that their homework was not finished because I made them turn off their lights at 1 A.M. and go to bed.

I assumed the blame for the gym clothes not being dry because I left them in the washer all night instead of setting the alarm and putting them in the dryer.

If a fork was bent, I got it.

If they yelled at me that they needed a note to get back into school after being ill and I didn't get it to them by the time they closed the front door, let it be on my conscience if they were sent home.

If I made them make their beds and they didn't have time to go to the bathroom, then all day their headache would be my fault.

If they dawdled and missed the school bus, it was my punishment to drive them to school and pick them up afterward.

After they had left I viewed all the food left on their plates. If I ate it, I went off my diet and was considered a bimbo. If I threw it away, I was wasteful and was considered a bad wife.

I was a cheap shot. Everyone knew it. I couldn't get out of a conversation without someone saying, "You paid full price for it?" "You carried the baby the full nine months?" "Get serious. You coudn't have gone through four years of college without learning how to play bridge." You didn't breast-feed? How tragic."

By the time I was thirty, I knew enough about guilt to start spreading a little of it myself. After all, how would my children know anything about it if I didn't set an example?

Since I had always been lousy at long speeches and shouting, I opted to use the nonverbal guilt medium. These forms have always been grossly underrated but are really quite effective.

I started out with the time-honored, no-fail, classic one: sighing.

Whenever one of the kids would fill up a glass to overflowing, I would sit there in absolute silence looking like I had just been told the rabbit died. Then slowly (don't hurry it) I would take a deep breath, deep enough to make my chest rise and get a catch in my throat, and then let it out slowly.

When this is done unhurriedly and with

feeling, you can just feel the rottenness of the accusee.

Another favorite was the pantomime with limited dialogue. It's a little dramatic, but it works. When one of my children informed me he was going on a picnic on Mother's Day with his friend's family, I would square my shoulders (this is important; it denotes courage) and give a very weak smile. Then without commenting one way or another, I'd go to the sewing basket and get a piece of black fabric and begin to drape his empty chair at the dinner table. (By this time he should be feeling so miserable he has the phone in his hand.) Now you're ready for the zinger. Smile painfully and say, "Have a good time, son."

My ace in the hole was the "I'll do it myself" number.

When I asked my husband or one of the children to take the garbage cans to the curb and they didn't respond right away, I'd paddle out in the darkness in a pair of bedroom slippers (preferably in the snow), a coat that didn't fit, no hat and no gloves, and begin to drag the cans noisily to the driveway inch by inch . . . HOLDING MY SIDE.

It was important in this operation to say little . . . just wince, strain, and occasionally yell to a neighbor, "How lucky you are to have people who love you."

One afternoon I announced to my husband and son that the television antenna had blown off course. No one moved. I rattled around in the garage for the ladder, dragged it to the side of the house, and slowly ascended to the roof. I must have sat up there three quarters of an hour waiting for someone to follow me. I had just confirmed my suspicion. Ruth was probably right. It was time to read *I'll Give Up Guilt When I Stop Making You Feel Rotten.*

The book was two years old, but it was still twenty years ahead of where I was. The author, Jim Preach, said it was time adults let go of traditions. Relationships were changing. The days when a family existed as a matched set were gone. Never had there been a time when individuals flourished and there was no need to feel guilty about its passing.

Already I felt better. Just knowing that I was no longer responsible for clean underwear if my son had an accident was a weight off my mind.

Jim also said that a lot of guilt stemmed from setting goals too high not only for yourself but for others. You cannot always agree, he said, but at least you can try to understand.

"If you're at odds with your children, don't make them feel guilty for their actions and yourself feel guilty because you don't agree, just keep lines of communication open and establish some kind of rapport."

It wasn't easy advice. Children and parents were living in different worlds. The new morality was like future shock and I couldn't get used to it. Could a girl who suffered from terminal contrite when she drove a boy to lust by wearing patent-leather pumps find happiness in a home where her kids watched *The Flying Nun* and figured they'd made their Easter duty?

I wasn't the only parent who felt it. We talked about it a lot. What we thought was a normal communication gap had become a cultural cavern that widened every day.

While parents prattled on about writing notes of thanks for graduation gifts, the kids weren't even planning on showing up for the ceremony.

While parents were rousting their kids out of bed and laying the responsibility for cutting the grass on them the kids were smoking it.

One afternoon I answered the phone. It was a girl asking for my son. In my time a girl never called a boy unless she was asked to pass on a homework assignment or was inviting him to the cotillion.

To show my displeasure at the custom, I sucked in my breath slowly in preparation for my "sighing" number. My son looked at me sharply and I smiled even when my face turned blue.

17

Contemporary Etiquette That's AWRIIITE

There's a special place in heaven for chaperones where the sun always shines, varicose veins dissipate, and the bar never closes.

I had enjoyed a self-exile from school activities for several years, mainly because I figured I had served my time. I had gone to camp and eaten raw chicken cooked over a tin can punched with holes, chaperoned a group of sixth-graders through a meat-packing plant, and sat through summers of Little League softball games that were real squeakers: Giants, 87–Dust Devils, 34.

When Mrs. Bitterly, the advisor of the senior class, called me to help chaperone the prom, I instinctively started to decline. Then I changed my mind.

I got out my trusty book of etiquette to brush up on what a chaperone did. It said: "The presence of an adult guards our young people from possible foolishness or from involving themselves in situations from which they are not mature enough to extract themselves."

That didn't sound so bad. And after all, what better way to understand today's young people than to spend an evening with them.

It's logic like that that fills nursing homes.

To begin with, my son said he wasn't going to the prom. It cost too much to rent a suit, the evening was a bore, and, besides, no girl had asked him yet.

Mrs. Bitterly called a meeting of the chaperones for the following Wednesday to fill us in on what to expect.

"If any of you has a hearing problem," she said, "let me know now."

A woman said, "I can hear perfectly."

"Then you may be excused," she said. "We are looking for people whose hearing is already impaired. By the end of the evening the music could conceivably make you lose your appetite, make you nauseated, or render you sterile. Those of you proficient in lipreading skills will do well.

"Now, we are doing away with the hand stamp this year. We used to stamp the hand of every guest at the prom. When they went out and came back the stamp showed up under a fluorescent lamp. However, last year, Mrs. Miller had trouble with a few older rowdies who crashed the party and had the stamp tattooed on their tongues. She didn't feel she should quarrel with this.

"I cannot stress enough: be sure of your authority. When you walk into the parking lot and discover three hoods who do not attend the school ripping off a car and have a tire iron in their hands, make sure you have a better threat than, 'You know this makes you ineligible for the Robert Frost poetry awards in the spring.'

"If you are going for a 'bust' of any kind, make sure you are familiar with the facts. Two years ago, a guidance counselor summoned an emergency unit, two police cruisers, and a priest for a boy who had just thrown two Tic Tacs into his mouth to improve his breath.

"You may dance if you like but know that the current craze is disco and if you do not have a flight plan filed, you could hurt yourself.

"Lastly, how do you know when the prom is over? First, there will be a ringing sensation in the ears and the band will be gone. Your eyes will no longer smart from Clearasil and your car will be the only one left in the parking lot . . . if you are lucky."

Personally, I thought Mrs. Bitterly overreacted. Other than the fact that for a few days following the prom I answered the phone and it wasn't ringing, I did fine. The kids seemed to have a good time. Maybe it was my success with the prom that prompted me to approach my son and ask him about his future.

"I've been checking into it," he said. On his desk were catalogues from every school you can imagine; none of them sounded familiar. I leafed through a few of them: Diablo Karate School . . . Electronics Institute and Tape Deck Installation . . . and College of Transcendental Bowling.

"Are you serious about these?"

"I've eliminated a lot of them," he said. "Especially the ones behind the Iron Curtain. Their football teams are lousy."

"Well, why don't we check out a few?" I said. "Your father and I could go along and we could make a vacation out of it."

I have spent better vacations in intensive care.

The first school was out because it was twenty miles from the ski slopes.

The second school was out because their football team lost six games the previous year.

The third school was out because they had a grading system.

The fourth school we looked at, he loved. I expected John Belushi to fly through a window any minute dressed in ham and cheese. The rooms looked like cells with terminal mildew. A girl in a bathrobe was walking her dog in the corridor. Someone was cooking illegal brownies.

"How many ironing boards do you have?" I asked.

A hush fell over the entire dorm.

"What are the posted hours that you have to be in at nights?"

A hush fell over the entire campus.

"Where is your house mother?"

A hush fell over the entire state.

They weren't guilt-stricken. They were all laughing themselves to death.

I couldn't pretend to be anything but confused over the change in relationships. "Roommate" had an entirely different connotation, as did "companion," "associate," and—as one of my daughter's friends listed

234

the unwed father on the birth certificate—
"significant other person."

I remember going to a wedding of the
daughter of a friend. The bride wore something old/something new/something bor-
rowed/something blue and it was the same
thing. A pair of jeans. She had met her husband when he was living with her girl friend.
I remember the organ played a hymnlike
melody that was hauntingly familiar. I
couldn't identify it. Then it came to me
while they were exchanging their vows. It
was "Days of Wine and Roses."

The next time I went to the library, I
asked if there was a book on modern man-
ners and morals and the librarian recommended *Contemporary Etiquette That's
Awriiite.*

In checking over the index, I discovered
things had changed since Amy Vanderbilt
recommended shaking hands with your
gloves on until your engagement had been
formally announced.

There was a chapter on dating: how

long does a boy keep a girl waiting until he finishes dressing.

Weddings: what to do when the groom is still married.

Entertaining: when to wear shoes and when to carry them.

Grooming: the six occasions in your life when you shave your legs.

Houseguests: explaining "meaningful relationships" to your sixty-five-year-old mother who insists on putting your roommate in a Big Boy recliner for the night.

Getting a job and other obscenities.

Introductions: explaining to a fourth-grade teacher why you have two sets of sons the same age who are related through divorce.

Why wouldn't children be different? Most had been conceived during a commercial break on the late-night movie, weaned on every new concept in education ever devised, nurtured on social change that affected the entire world, and sustained on a diet of sex, violence, realism, and independence.

Who would have thought that I would be sitting in a movie with my high school son and when the sex in the movie reached gasping proportions, he would lean over to me and say, "Why don't you go out for some more popcorn, Mom?"

That was my line when he asked which one of the dwarfs was Snow White's husband.

Who would have guessed after twenty-five years of vitamins, shots, and regular checkups that your children would accuse you of poisoning them with bleached flour, sugar, additives, and butterfat and would sit around telling you in explicit detail how hot dogs are made?

For a while after I leafed through the book I took on a new air. Whenever my son mentioned something that was supposed to shock me I responded with "Really!" or "Awriiite" or "Far out."

There was nothing that could shake me up. If he related a particularly grim movie to me I shouted, "Go for it." If he played a

237

record at 97 decibels I yelled, "Could you turn that up? I love the words."

If he told me he skipped a day at school, I took a deep breath and said, "You're not the only one."

Finally one day he said he was not going to get a job this summer because he wanted time to get in touch with his feelings and find out where he was coming from.

I changed into a parent right before his eyes.

"I don't know where you're coming from," I shouted. "But I know where you're headed. The same place you were last summer . . . getting up at the crack of noon. Every time I shook out the bedclothes, there you were. Every time I walked in front of the TV set, there you were. Every time I followed the beam of light from the refrigerator door, you were at the end of it.

"For your information, Peter Pan, you are getting a job this summer. Say it slowly at first . . . let it roll over your tongue and you'll get used to it . . . j o b . . . J O B . . . JOB. It's an old establishment expression meaning to have some pride in yourself, some productivity, pulling your own weight, having a reason for getting up in the morning and being tired enough to go to sleep at night.

"For someone who abhors materialism, you sure demand a lot of it . . . for someone who is turned off by pollution, you sure contribute to it. For someone who is a pacifist, you sure know how to start an internal family war. So, get off your duff tomorrow and get a job!"

My son didn't say anything for a full minute. He just smiled and shook his head. Then he said, "You talk pretty good."

"What do you mean by a crack like that?"

"I mean all this time all you ever did was look at me and frown and sigh a lot. I never knew what you were thinking. I just felt rotten."

"You mean you don't feel rotten now?"

"Yeah, but now I know *why* I feel rotten. I never knew before."

"I guess old Jim Preach was right."

"Are you still plowing through all those self-help books?"

"Don't knock 'em. Someday I'll get it all together."

"You know what your trouble is," said my son. "You try too hard. You're going through the old 'Be a winner' routine. When I was younger, I used to think winning was everything. It isn't. Don't sweat it. Just lay back and let it happen. Take life as it comes. The important thing to remember is Be Yourself."

A few hours later he brushed by me in the kitchen. He was wearing his father's tennis shorts, a T-shirt he filched from the school's lost and found, and carried his brother's tennis racket. He grabbed my car keys off the countertop and winked. "Remember what I said. Be yourself!"

18

I Don't Care What I Say . . . I Still Like Me

It had been all of three months since I picked up a how-to book.

A lot of people I know eased off reading them gradually, but I knew if I was to kick the habit I'd have to stop reading them cold turkey and live just one day at a time.

It wasn't easy. I was surrounded by social self-help readers who couldn't wait to pick up a volume and offer me one. Tonight would be my first big test.

We were going to a cocktail party at Jill's house. My husband hated cocktail parties. He said people drank too much and it was like talking to a traffic light . . . a blinking red eye, and in five seconds they sped off to another corner.

I felt pretty wonderful. My daughter was giving up television for Lent this year instead of me. My older son had shaved and no longer looked like a Lincoln penny, and that very day we had just gotten a letter from our younger son at school (*Mom* was spelled with two o's, but what the heck, he was only a freshman).

The entire family was pleased that I had stopped improving myself and was back to my old ways. I loved everyone else better than me, was insecure about my job, had no idea what I was feeling or why and almost never listened to my body.

There had been withdrawal symptoms after I had stopped reading self-help books. I knew there would be. I was checking out in a supermarket one day when I glanced down at a headline near the checkout stand. The article was topped by IT'S 11 O'CLOCK! DO YOU KNOW WHERE YOUR ANXIETIES ARE?

My palms became sweaty, my throat

dry, and instinctively I dug into my handbag for my glasses. My husband came by just in time, steered me toward the door and said, "You need a drink."

It was strange standing in the middle of Jill's living room. I couldn't help but reflect this was where it all began . . . exactly one year ago.

A voice at my elbow interrupted my thoughts. "Hi! Have a drink?"

It was Phyllis.

"Of course," I smiled.

"How about a cheese fluff?"

"Thanks."

"How about a book on *Can You Handle Your Biofeedback During a Full Moon?*"

"Good-bye Phyllis."

"Wait a minute!" she shouted. "Even the Pope approves biorhythms."

"I don't care if they're at the top of the charts, I am not going to get involved in another self-help book."

"As you stand there talking," said Phyllis, "your frustrations, your tensions, and your conflict translate into specific events taking place inside your body."

"I am leaving you, Phyllis. You're going to look like a fool standing here talking to yourself."

"God forbid your biorhythms could be out of sync, but it happens. You could be in one of your critical days. There's always the possibility you could meet with a freak accident."

"I am just saying good-bye to one."

"Why are you so sore?" she persisted.

"Because ever since you turned me on to *The Sub-Total Woman*, my life has not been the same."

"Then it's true. You are having trouble with your marriage."

Rita overheard our conversation and said, "Listen, sweetie, Dan and I swear by the Camp of the Close Encounter and Massage Village about fifty miles north of here. It's a wonderful shared experience of personal learning. And you don't have to worry about a wardrobe—if you get my drift."

"No, really, Rita, our marriage is just fine. The kids have all left home and ..."

"Did I hear you say you're going through the Empty Nest trauma?" asked Natalie. "Some people make the transition smoothly, but you're going to have to be careful. You're a child-geared person. We've always known that. You were always fulfilled by kids ... baking the funny cakes for their birthdays, buying a bolt of material and dressing them all alike like wallpaper, and you always had a sign in front of your house for as long as I can remember: FREE KITTENS. Have you read *Nest of Tears: Handling a Child's Rejection?*"

"Natalie, listen to me. I am not rejected. At my age it's predictable ..."

"Listen to her," said Marcia. "At her age. Why, I've got a cookie sheet older than you. Don't be so insecure. You're not all that unattractive. Nothing that reading *Look Like a Million Dollars for Only Half That Amount* couldn't cure."

I reached out and grabbed *Can You*

Handle Your Biofeedback During a Full Moon? and ran my hand over the cover. I could feel beads of perspiration on my forehead and my hand shook. Could I stand to have it start all over again?

The raising of my consciousness level seemed so innocent at first I promised myself I could stop raising it anytime I wanted to.

The lies about how many self-help books I was reading a day.

The excuses I made when I sat at the breakfast table and read just a few more pages from *How to Get Rich During a Democratic Administration* before I could start my housework.

The day my husband found *Suppressing My Primal Scream* hidden in my hosiery drawer.

The night I had too much to read and embarrassed my family by standing on a coffee table reciting from *How to Engage in Perversion as a Hobby.*

Did I want to go back to that?

I handed the book back to Phyllis. "Thanks, but no thanks. I am going to be myself."

"You're kidding," said Marcia. "Without any help from anyone?"

"That's right."

"You're going against the tide," said Natalie. "No one is themselves these days. It just isn't good enough. Everyone is into some kind of a transitional flow."

"You're copping out," snapped Phyllis. "Sure, it's easy to sit around and just let things happen, but the bottom line is groping! How can you be happy if you're not miserable?"

Natalie was right about one thing. I was out of the mainstream. There were "color parties" in which everyone in the neighborhood was invited to be analyzed and effective colors were suggested for them to wear and to decorate their homes with. But no one asked me.

A speaker at Town Hall discussed how to survive an audit from the IRS using tranquilizers that you could buy over the counter, but I wasn't invited.

Phyllis even gave a party for all dogs who were born under the Gemini sign. My dog was the only Gemini in the block who wasn't there.

I didn't see any of them until one day in the book department I looked up and there was Phyllis.

She was holding a book called *I Don't Care What I Say . . . I Still Like Me*. She seemed surprised to see me.

"So how's Polly Perfect? Still handling your own anxiety attacks, struggling with your birth traumas, and treating your neuroses out of your medicine cabinet?"

"I'm doing okay," I smiled.

"I suppose it's a waste of time to point out that this new book is a brilliant insight into the Id? It tells how through conscientious self-analysis a person can achieve happiness without a lot of inner conflict and mythological mishmash. It facilitates and utilizes an entirely new concept in living experience."

"That translates to 'be yourself.' Right?"

Phyllis looked surprised. "Right. Did you read it?"

"Phyllis," I smiled, "I wrote it."

Author's Note:
The Pursuit
of Happiness

Our forefathers didn't know what they were laying on us when they penned the Declaration of Independence.

Life and Liberty were pieces of cake compared to the Pursuit of Happiness.

I have lived this book for over a year and never knew how miserable I was until I tried to find out why I was happy. Oh, I knew I was bored, depressed, neurotic, inhibited and unfulfilled, but I figured no one is perfect.

During the last year I have come to grips with midlife, found inner peace, fought outer flab, interpreted my fantasies, examined my motives for buying, dissected my marriage, charted my astrological stars, and become my best AND ONLY friend. I have brought order to my life, meditated, given up guilt, adjusted to the new morality, and spent every living hour understanding me, interpreting me, and loving me—and you know what? I'm bored to death with me. If I never hear another word about me it will be too soon.

I have no more curiosity about myself. No more drive to make me a better person. No more patience to find out what I am feeling.

If I never see the words "input," "concept," "feedback," or "bottom line," it will be all right with me.

If I ever say the words "share with you" or "at this point of time in my life," I hope my saliva runs dry.

After a year of reading sixty-two self-help books and articles, I have discovered something interesting. You don't find happiness. It finds you.

If you are married, you're supposed to be happier than those who are not. If you control your life and have the wherewithal to do it, you're supposed to be happier. If you love and are loved back you're supposed to be happier. Financial security will make you happier (I've suspected that for a long time).

I have discovered something else. We are not permitted to be depressed any more, nor are we allowed to age.

Already people are beginning to wonder where have all the old people gone? They've gone underground because we live in a time when we must go through life like a miracle fabric: drip-dry and wrinkle-free. If your hands look as young as your married daughter's, you can get on a commercial. If you are seventy and can do a time step, you get a shot on the Carson show. If you saw the Civil War and can wave a flag, you get a standing ovation.

The "Is Everybody Happy?" syndrome is just as bad. I used to wallow—no, nearly drown—in wonderful funky days of despair when nothing went right, and I loved it. Those down-in-the-dirty-pits days when I was unappreciated, overworked, underpaid, and had split heels from not wearing socks in the winter.

I couldn't win. My hair wouldn't curl. The hot water heater rusted out. My best friend's husband got a promotion. My child dropped a typewriter that belonged to the school. Someone asked me if my youngest was my grandchild. The car door froze shut on my morning to drive.

Maybe those days were why I appreciated the ones where my gynecologist said I just had flu, and the dryer only needed a fifteen-cent fuse.

This book is not a put-down of all self-help books. It focuses on the absurdity of paying $12.95 for a cookbook that tells you how to save money. It points out how ludicrous it is to read a book on guilt that threatens, "If you don't read this, you'll regret it for the rest of your life." It takes on the books that take 362 pages to tell you,

"Stop listening to advice and take control of your own life."

After reading sixty-two books and articles on how to deal with oneself, I realized something was missing . . . a sense of humor. I cannot believe that people look into the mirror that reflects their actions and behavior and keep a straight face.

There is a paragraph from Gail Sheehy's *Passages* that seems to sum up a flaw most of us have when we pursue happiness: "Would that there were an award for people who come to understand the concept of enough. Good enough. Successful enough. Thin enough. Rich enough. Socially responsible enough. When you have self-respect you have enough, and when you have enough, you have self-respect."

Aunt Erma's Cope Book fulfills a fantasy for me. I always wanted to be an authority on how to do something . . . ANYTHING! For years, I watched the Dr. Joyces, the Dear Abbys, the Mrs. Clarabelles, and the Miss Americas come to grips with the problems of life head-on.

After a year of research, it became apparent to me—the only "how-to" book I had enough expertise to write was "How to Get from Monday to Friday in 12 Days."

In her infinite wisdom, my mother offered yet another observation on my months of self-examination, devotion to improvement, and quest for happiness. She said, "I'll be glad when you hit menopause. It'll take your mind off your problems."